INTRODUCTION

People often confuse apes and monkeys, using both words interchangeably. Apes and monkeys, however, are two different groups of animals. The confusion is perhaps understandable because they have several similar features, and there are only a few differences that can separate the two. Both animals can be found swinging through the trees in a lush rainforest or be seen lazing in shady spots, grooming each other in large groups.

SPIDER MONKEY

These monkeys and most other New World monkeys have a fifth limb, as well as their arms and legs. Their long tails are prehensile, and the monkeys wrap them around a branch to provide extra support. Like the palm of a hand or foot, the inside surface of the tail is bald, without the thick fur that covers the body. This makes the tail better at gripping. New World monkeys can even hang from just their tail, leaving their hands and feet free.

All apes and monkeys are primates, which are a group of mammals that also includes many other small tree-living animals called prosimians. Lemurs and bush babies are two members of this third group. There is, however, one other member of the primate group: humans. The first primates were most like the prosimians we see today. Like apes, monkeys and all other modern primates, these primitive relations did not have claws. Instead they had nails on the tips of their fingers. These allowed them to hold objects with a finer and more delicate grip than their less nimble mammal cousins. The monkeys and apes that evolved later were even better at holding food and other things in their hands.

Most primates live in trees, and so their clawless hands and feet are also good at gripping even the flimsiest of branches. Living in a tree is a complicated business. To get food, primates have to pick their way through a mind-boggling network of swaying branches and death-defying leaps. One wrong step or a single miscalculated jump could lead to a long and fatal fall down to the forest floor below. Therefore, primates have to be clever enough to make all the complicated decisions needed to stay alive. Prosimians are clever compared to most mammals, but monkeys and apes are very brainy in comparison. They are good problem-solvers, especially the apes, and live in elaborate societies.

CHIMPANZEE

Humans are unique animals because we use our brains to work out how to survive in any habitat. We usually achieve this by altering the environment to suit our needs, such as by building houses or turning forests into farms. Although other species of apes, such as this chimpanzee, are extremely intelligent, they do not have this ability to help them survive. Due to the many changes people have made to the natural world, all of the great apes are now very rare and in danger of dying out completely.

Humans, the cleverest of all primates, share more features with apes than monkeys, and we are often grouped together with them. Apart from humans, there are 15 other kinds or species of ape. Eleven of these are the gibbons, or the so-called lesser apes. These apes live in the forests of South-east Asia. The remaining four species are the great apes: the chimpanzee, bonobo, gorilla and orang-utan. The first three great apes live in Central Africa, while the orang-utan is found on some Indonesian islands. Just like people, apes do not have tails. This is the easiest way to tell an ape from a monkey, since all monkeys (and prosimians) have at least some kind of tail.

There are more than 170 species of monkey. They live alongside apes and prosimians in Africa and Asia, but they can also be found in South America, and they are the only primates in the region. The monkeys that live in South America, part of the so-called New World, are different to those that live in the Old World — Asia and Africa. New World monkeys include capuchins and howlers, while baboons and proboscis monkeys are examples of Old World monkeys. New World monkeys have grasping prehensile tails and they spend their lives swinging around in the trees of humid jungles. Old World monkeys are much more diverse. Many live in the trees, but some species make their home on the ground, often out in the open.

SILVERBACK GORILLA

Gorillas are the largest of all primates. Like most of the great apes, these leaf-eating giants live in social groups called troops. Gorilla troops are run by a tough, older male. While older people sometimes hide their grey hairs with dye, the gorilla leader's silver-grey hair is an important sign of dominance and his capability to survive.

LEMUR

These primates live on the island of Madagascar. There are no monkeys or apes on this island, but a variety of lemurs fill the trees instead. Lemurs have longer bodies and shorter legs than monkeys and apes, which makes them look more like cats or large squirrels. Lemurs do not exist anywhere else in the world, so most kinds of lemur are now very rare.

BABOON TROOP

Most monkeys and apes can only survive in a thick forest, but a few species, such as these baboons, have evolved to be able to survive out in the open. Baboons travel long distances each day to collect food. They travel in large troops because there is safety in numbers – if they are attacked, the male baboons will stand and fight while the females and young monkeys make a retreat.

THE WORLD OF APES

When coming eye to eye with a great ape it is hard not to feel that you are being studied in the same way you are studying the ape. Great apes are our closest relatives. We share more than 99 per cent of our genes with chimpanzees and bonobos, for example. However, that fraction of one per cent makes us very different from each other.

What is a Great Ape?

The four great apes – the chimpanzee, bonobo, gorilla and orang-utan – look similar to us because they are our closest animal relatives. Humans are sometimes called the fifth great ape. The great apes are closely related to the lesser apes, called gibbons. Nearly 99 per cent of our genes are the same as those of a chimpanzee. In fact, chimpanzees are more closely related to humans than they are to gorillas. Like us, the other great apes are intelligent, use tools, solve problems and communicate. They can also learn a language, although their vocal cords cannot produce the right range of sounds to speak.

▼ APE FEATURES
Gorillas are the largest of the great apes. Typical ape features include long arms (longer than their legs), flexible wrist joints, gripping thumbs and fingers, and no tail. Apes are clever, with big brains.

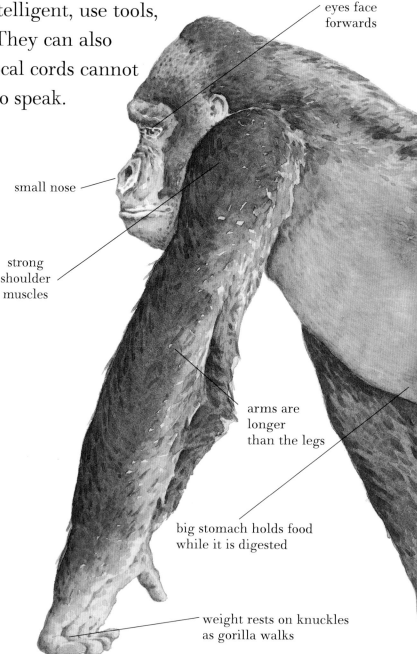

eyes face forwards

small nose

strong shoulder muscles

arms are longer than the legs

big stomach holds food while it is digested

weight rests on knuckles as gorilla walks

▲ RED APE
Red, shaggy orang-utans are the largest tree-living animals in the world. Their name means person-of-the-forest. Orang-utans live on the islands of Borneo and Sumatra in South-east Asia.

▲ STUDYING APES

Much of what we know today about wild apes is based on the work of scientists such as Dr Dian Fossey, who spent many years carefully observing gorillas in the wild.

GROUPS ▶

Family groups of between five and forty gorillas live together in the misty rainforests and mountains of central Africa. Each group is led by an adult male. He decides where the group will feed, sleep and travel.

apes do not have a tail

feet rest flat on the ground

King Kong

At the beginning of the 1930s, the film King Kong *showed a giant gorilla as a dangerous monster. In the movie, a team of hunters capture Kong and take him to America. We now know that gorillas are peaceful animals, very different from the movie monster.*

▼ APE FACES

Have you ever watched a chimpanzee in a zoo and found that it has turned to watch you? Great apes are often as interested in watching us, as we are in watching them.

Ape Shapes and Sizes

It's hard to believe that a tiny new-born gorilla, half the weight of most human babies, may grow up to be a heavyweight male that weighs nearly 200kg. Gorillas are the largest of the four great apes, while chimpanzees and bonobos are the smallest – similar in size to a 12-year-old boy or girl. Male great apes are up to twice the size and weight of females. This helps them to frighten predators and rivals. However, male and female gibbons are the same size. They are much smaller than the great apes and so are known as the lesser apes. Their small size allows them to live high in the trees all the time. Large male gorillas are too heavy for a permanent treetop lifestyle, although they do climb trees for fruit and buds.

▲ **SMALL APE**
Male chimpanzees stand just under 1.5m tall and weigh up to 40kg. Females are a little shorter and lighter. Chimpanzees have muscular bodies and are strong for their size.

orang-utan
(Pongo pygmaeus)

◄ **BIG FACE**
A fully grown male orang-utan has fatty pads the size of dinner plates on his cheeks. They make him look bigger and help him to frighten off rival males.

▲ **SIZE DIFFERENCE**
Male gorillas are up to twice the size of females. A wild male gorilla stands about 1.8m tall and is incredibly muscular. A female gorilla is shorter – about 1.5m – and weighs about 90kg.

bonobo or pygmy chimpanzee
(Pan paniscus)

◄ A NEW SPECIES

Bonobos used to be known as pygmy chimpanzees but they were recognized as a separate species in 1929. Bonobos are about the same height as chimpanzees at the shoulder but they have a more slender and leggy body. Bonobos also have smaller, rounder heads when compared to chimpanzees. The hair on a bonobo's head usually looks as if it has been parted down the middle.

Did you know? A big male orang-utan is the weight of a heavyweight boxer.

► LESSER APE

The gibbons are the smallest and lightest of the apes. Most gibbons measure just over 60cm in length and weigh less than 7kg. There are 11 species of gibbon. The heaviest species is the siamang – the males weigh up to 14kg.

Yeti and Bigfoot

Some people believe that an ape-man lives hidden in the high mountains of Asia and the wilderness areas of North America. It is called a Yeti or the Abominable Snowman in the Himalayas and Bigfoot or Sasquatch in North America.

white-cheeked gibbon
(Hylobates concolor leucogenys)

Ape Habitats

If you want to see wild apes in their natural habitats, you have to travel to tropical Africa or South-east Asia. Most apes live in tropical rainforests, but some chimpanzees are found in more open, deciduous woodlands or in wooded grasslands, and some gorillas prefer mountain forests with their lush vegetation and misty atmosphere. In some places, gibbons live in deciduous forests, too. All the apes used to be more widespread, but over time, they are being gradually squeezed into smaller and smaller areas as people have hunted them and destroyed their habitats.

▲ VANISHING APE
In the dark and dappled rainforest where orang-utans live, their shaggy, orange hair blends in with the tangle of forest plants. This makes them surprisingly difficult to see.

GORILLA SIGNS ▶
It is often hard for scientists to watch gorillas in their forest habitats. Instead, the scientists study the signs left behind by the gorillas as they move about.

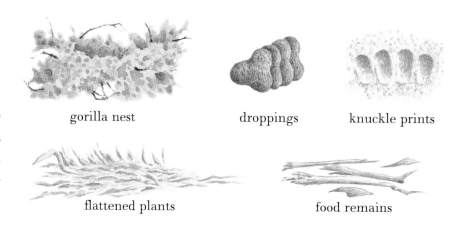

gorilla nest

droppings

knuckle prints

flattened plants

food remains

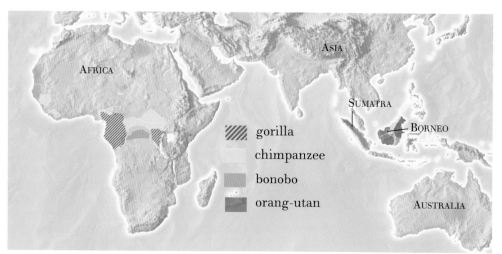

◀ WHERE APES LIVE
Gorillas, chimpanzees and bonobos live in Africa and orang-utans live only on the islands of Borneo and Sumatra. However, orang-utans once lived in parts of mainland South-east Asia. Some people believe that they were hunted out by poachers.

ASIA

AFRICA

SUMATRA

BORNEO

gorilla

chimpanzee

bonobo

orang-utan

AUSTRALIA

▲ ROUTE MAP

Chimpanzees travel around their own neighbourhoods on the ground, following a network of paths. They use a mental map in their heads to decide where to go. Each day they work out where to get a good meal, climbing trees to find fruit and leaves, or to chase prey.

▲ TREETOP APE

Gibbons are totally at home in the tops of the trees and hardly ever go down to the ground. They are the only apes that do not build nests. They sleep sitting up in the forks of branches, resting on tough sitting pads. These pads act as built-in cushions.

▼ NIGHT NESTS

Every night, the adult great apes make nests in the trees or on the ground. They bend and weave together leafy branches and pile more leaves and branches on top. This makes a warm, springy nest to keep out the cold.

▲ MOUNTAIN HOME

Mountain gorillas live in dense, misty forests up to about 3,500m above sea level. At night, the temperature sometimes drops to below freezing but the long hair of the mountain gorillas helps them to keep warm.

chimpanzee
(Pan troglodytes)

Focus on

It's 6:30 in the morning. A group of gorillas is waking up. They are hungry after their night-time fast and reach out to pick a leafy breakfast in bed. Then the gorillas move off through the forest, feeding as they go. After a morning spent munching plants, they build day nests on the ground and take a rest for a couple of hours. This gives them time to digest their food and socialize. They are mountain gorillas. They live amid the beautiful and misty volcanic Virunga Mountains in Africa. They have lowland cousins who live in the tropical rainforests of eastern and western Central Africa.

CAREFUL CLIMBERS

Gorillas climb with great care and feel most secure when all four limbs are in contact with a branch. Young gorillas are lighter and often play by hanging beneath branches and swinging like a gibbon.

MOUNTAIN REFUGE

In 1925, the home of the mountain gorillas on the slopes of the Virunga volcanoes was declared Africa's first national park. The word *virunga* comes from a local expression meaning isolated mountains that reach the clouds. The Virunga mountains include both active and dormant volcanoes, but the gorillas live only on the dormant volcanoes.

LOWLAND GORILLAS

Travelling through the Odzala Forest, these western lowland gorillas feed in a swampy glade. Like all gorillas, they walk on all fours.

Gorilla Habitats

GORILLA CHAMPION

From her hut on Mount Visoke, Dian Fossey devoted herself to studying and protecting mountain gorillas. She began her work in 1967, winning the trust of the gorillas, studying their family relationships and making discoveries about their behaviour.

CLOUD FORESTS

Mists often swirl around the forests where the mountain gorillas live, so they are called cloud forests. Mosses and lichens grow well in the cool, damp air, and hang on the branches like untidy green hair.

LOWLAND FORESTS

Eastern lowland gorillas live in the dense lowland rainforests of eastern Congo. These forests are less open than the mountain gorillas' habitat, so it is more difficult for people to study lowland gorillas.

FOOD FOR FREE

On the rainy slopes where they live, the mountain gorillas have a wide variety of food, such as wild celery, bedstraw, bamboo shoots, thistles, brambles and nettles.

Bodies and Bones

A characteristic feature of great apes is their long, strong arms and flexible shoulders, which they use to clamber through the trees. They do not have tails to help them balance and grip the branches. Instead of hooves or paws, apes have hands and feet that can grasp branches and hold food very well. On the ground, an ape's strong arms and fingers take its weight as it walks on all fours. Humans are different from the other apes as they have short arms and long legs. Human arms are about 30 per cent shorter than human legs. Our bodies and bones are also designed for walking upright rather than for swinging through the trees. All the apes have a large head, with a big skull inside, to protect an intelligent brain.

◀ **APE SKELETON**
One of the notable features of an ape skeleton is the large skull that surrounds and protects the big brain. Apes also have long, strong finger and toe bones for gripping branches. The arm bones of the orang-utans, gorillas and chimpanzees are also extended, making their arms longer than their legs.

Did you know? Female orang-utans can weigh up to 36kg but males can weigh over 90kg.

▼ **THE BIG FIVE**
Great apes have similar bodies, although a human's body is less hairy and muscular than the bodies of the other apes. The main differences between ape bodies lie in the shape of the skull and the length of the arms and legs. Orang-utans have extra long arms to hang from branches, while humans have long legs for walking upright.

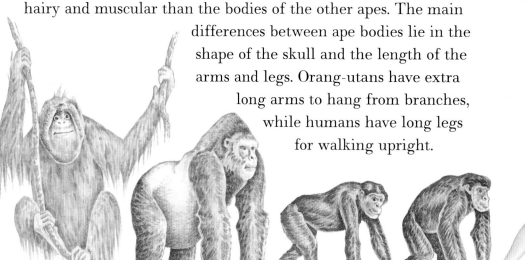

orang-utan   gorilla   bonobo   chimpanzee   human

16

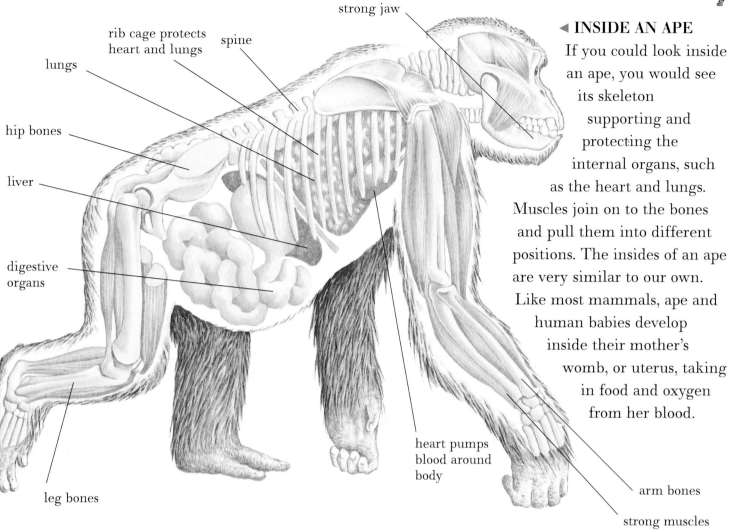

lungs

rib cage protects heart and lungs

spine

strong jaw

hip bones

liver

digestive organs

leg bones

heart pumps blood around body

arm bones

strong muscles

◀ **INSIDE AN APE**
If you could look inside an ape, you would see its skeleton supporting and protecting the internal organs, such as the heart and lungs. Muscles join on to the bones and pull them into different positions. The insides of an ape are very similar to our own. Like most mammals, ape and human babies develop inside their mother's womb, or uterus, taking in food and oxygen from her blood.

▲ **NO TAIL**
Apes, such as chimpanzees, do not have tails, but most monkeys do. Apes clamber and hang by their powerful arms. Monkeys walk along branches on all fours, using the tail for balance.

EXTRA HAND ▶
Many of the monkeys that live in the dense rainforests of Central and South America have special gripping tails, called prehensile tails. The tails also have sensitive tips that work like an extra one-fingered hand, allowing them to cling to the branches when gathering fruit.

western lowland gorilla
(Gorilla gorilla gorilla)

Hairy Apes

Apes are mammals, like cats, bears, mice and deer. Mammals are warm-blooded animals, and most have hair-covered bodies. The hair grows out of little pits in the skin called follicles, forming a layer that traps warm air given off by the body. This helps to keep an ape warm. Apes that live in colder places, such as mountain gorillas, have longer, thicker hair for extra warmth. Apes don't like the rain because their hair is not very waterproof. Sometimes apes try to shelter from the rain or make umbrellas out of large leaves, but often they just sit hunched up waiting for the rain to stop. Male and female chimpanzees both have black hair and all orang-utans have orange-red coats, whereas adult male gorillas have a distinctive silver back, and some male and female gibbons are totally different colours.

▲ **SILVER LEADER**

When a male gorilla is about 11 or 12 years old, he grows a saddle-shaped area of silvery grey hair on his back, and long, shaggy hair on his arms. He also loses his chest hair. He is called a silverback, and these changes show he is grown-up. Males whose hair has not yet changed are called blackbacks.

GROOMING ▶

Chimpanzees regularly search through each other's hair with their fingers, carefully picking out any dirt and lice, and cleaning cuts and scratches. Grooming feels pleasant and helps the apes to relax and reassure each other. It also helps to strengthen friendships.

18

◄ COLOUR CONTRAST

In some species of gibbon, males and females have different coloured hair. For instance, male concolor and hoolock gibbons are black, while females are a golden colour. Male and female lar gibbons are the same colour, but populations living in different places may be various colours.

white-handed gibbons
(Hylobates lar)

▲ GOING GREY

Chimpanzees can live for 40 or 50 years. As a chimpanzee grows older, its coat fades and may turn grey. Its hair also thins and older chimps may start to go bald.

orang-utan
(Pongo pygmaeus)

LONG HAIR ►

Orang-utans from Sumatra have longer, thicker hair than those from Borneo. Scientists now think that they are a separate species from their Bornean relatives. Sumatran males have shaggy faces, with long, rich beards and moustaches that extend on to their cheeks. Even female Sumatran orang-utans have impressive chin hair. The long hair of male orang-utans makes them look bigger and so helps to scare off rivals.

▲ HAIRY SIGNALS

This chimpanzee has made its hair stand on end to make itself look bigger and more frightening. A nervous or fearful chimp has flattened hair and a 'fear grin'.

Hands and Feet

Can you imagine how difficult it would be to pick something up if your arms ended in paws, hooves or flippers? It would be impossible to grip the object and you could not turn it around, carry it, throw it, pull it apart or put it together. An ape's hands and feet are remarkable. They are very adaptable, and the opposing thumb or big toe enables them to grasp firmly or hold delicately. Ape hands and feet are strong and flexible, allowing apes to climb, swing and jump through the treetops. They also allow apes to reach food, investigate their surroundings, build nests and groom their family and friends. In most apes, the feet look very much like hands, but in humans, the feet look different. This is because human feet are adapted for walking rather than climbing.

▲ **SMILE, PLEASE**
Grasping a delicate camera lens, a gorilla demonstrates how it can pick up fragile objects without breaking them. A gorilla has thicker, sturdier hands than a person, with fingers the size of bananas and a smaller thumb. Its hands have to be strong so that they can support the weight of the gorilla's body when it walks around on all fours.

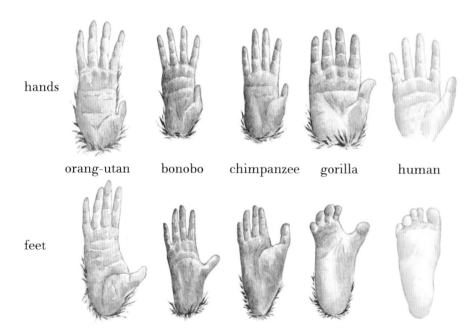

hands

orang-utan   bonobo   chimpanzee   gorilla   human

feet

◄ **LOOK-ALIKE HANDS**
The hands of the great apes have several features in common, such as nails and long, sensitive fingers. The thumb on a great ape's hand goes off at an angle and can press against each finger. The big toe on an ape's foot can also do this, except in humans. Bonobos have a unique feature not shared by the other apes — webbing between the second and third toes.

orang-utan
(Pongo pygmaeus)

Did you know? Humans have over 5 million hairs on their bodies.

▲ OPPOSABLE THUMB

Since a great ape's thumb can easily touch, or oppose, its fingers, it is called an opposable thumb. This special thumb gives an ape's hand a precise pincer grip, allowing it to pick up objects as small as berries.

▲ GRAPPLING IRONS

An orang-utan's arms and legs end in huge hands and feet that work like powerful grabs. Just one hand or foot can take the entire weight of the ape.

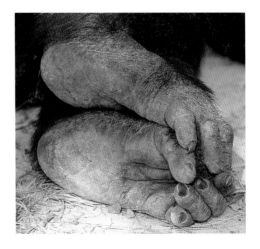

▲ HAND-FOOT

Unlike a human, a chimp can use its feet rather like hands, to hold and investigate things. The opposable big toe stretches out around one side of a branch while the toes reach around the other side, giving a very strong grip.

▲ FLAT FEET

Chimpanzees are flat-footed, with tough, hairless feet and long toes. When upright, their feet have to take all of the body weight.

Walking and Climbing

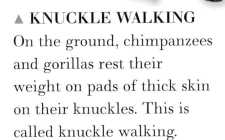

To an ape, the tangle of trunks, branches and vines in a forest are like a gigantic climbing frame that provides high-level walkways through the air. Gibbons, orang-utans and bonobos spend a lot of time in the trees. Large male orang-utans also travel on the ground some of the time because of their great weight. The true masters of treetop travel are the gibbons, able to leap and swing effortlessly across gaps at great speed and at great heights. Chimpanzees and gorillas are mainly ground-based creatures, although chimpanzees are equally at home in the trees or on the ground. Gorillas, even with their bulk, are amazingly agile (if somewhat careful) climbers.

▲ **KNUCKLE WALKING**

On the ground, chimpanzees and gorillas rest their weight on pads of thick skin on their knuckles. This is called knuckle walking.

▲ **CLIMBING CHIMP**

Chimpanzees climb into the trees to find leaves or fruit to eat, to chase prey and to build sleeping nests. Their long fingers hook over the branches and give them a good grip for both climbing and swinging.

Tarzan of the Apes
American writer Edgar Rice Burroughs created the character Tarzan in a magazine story published in 1912. Tarzan was orphaned as a baby in the jungles of Africa. A tribe of great apes takes care of him, teaching him how to survive in the jungle and swing through trees. He shares his later adventures with his wife Jane and their son Korak.

orang-utans
(*Pongo pygmaeus*)

◀ FLEXIBLE APE

The body weight of an orang-utan is evenly shared between its arms and legs. This helps the orang-utan to keep its balance. The shoulder and hip joints of an orang-utan are very supple, allowing it to stretch easily between branches. Orang-utans can even eat hanging upside-down. They can sway slender trees until they can reach far enough to catch a branch on the next tree. They often make a lot of noise crashing through the trees.

Did you know? A gorilla can run at 25-33km/h over short distances.

◀ SWINGING GIBBONS

With their extraordinarily long arms, gibbons swing at breathtaking speed from branch to branch, often leaping huge distances. Special wrist bones allow a gibbon to turn its body as it swings without loosening its grip. This means it can swing hand-over-hand in a speedy swing, known as brachiating. Compared with the noisy crashings of monkeys leaping from tree to tree, gibbons are almost silent travellers.

▲ GRIPPING FEAT

Gorillas are wary tree climbers and rarely swing by their arms like chimps or gibbons. They climb down from a tree backwards, holding the trunk loosely with both feet in a controlled slide.

23

Did you know? Gorilla skulls were used in ceremonies to give people the power of the gorilla.

Skulls and Teeth

An ape's skull is a hard casing of fused bones that surrounds and protects the large brain. The structure of the skull shows that an ape depends more on sight than smell as a means of gathering information about the outside world. The eyes are enclosed in bony sockets and are positioned on the front of the face. Since the sense of smell is less important, the face is flattened, with a smaller space for the nose. An ape's jaws are relatively well developed with 32 teeth – large, broad molars at the back, shovel-shaped incisors at the front for cutting, and pointed canines in-between. The long canines can be used as weapons and when nervous, apes yawn to display them. In addition, chimpanzees will sometimes make use of sticks and stones as weapons.

◄ **OPEN WIDE**

Gorillas have broad, flat molar teeth at the back of their mouths. These teeth grind, crush and chew tough seeds and roots, such as nuts and wild ginger. Sharp, pointed canine teeth are used for tearing food. Males have large canine teeth that may be used for threat displays, or for fighting.

GORILLA POWER

powerful jaws and cheek teeth for chewing tough vegetation

strong, rounded skull of the female gorilla

A gorilla has the largest skull of all the apes. The female skull is strong and robust to protect them from blows.. Male gorillas and some large females have bony ridges on the top of the skull called sagittal crests. The big muscles that move the lower jaw are attached to the crest.

BRAINY CHIMP

although chimpanzees eat meat, their teeth suggest that their ancestors' diet was mainly vegetarian

Like a gorilla, a chimpanzee also has a strong jaw and protective bony ridges above the eyes. But its skull is thinner and not as robust as that of a gorilla. However, inside its skull, a chimpanzee has a much bigger brain than a gorilla in comparison to its body size.

ORANG-UTAN

crushing cheek teeth, for grinding fruit and leaves

The skull of an orang-utan slopes back more than the skulls of the other great apes, and the bony ridges around the eye sockets are less well developed. Like male gorillas, the big male orang-utans have bony crests on the top of the skull for the attachment of large jaw muscles.

LITTLE GIBBON

dagger-like canines for fighting and display

Gibbons have much smaller bodies than the other apes, so their skulls are also smaller and more lightly built. There is little difference between the size of the skulls of male and female gibbons. A gibbon's skull is more rounded than those of the other apes.

Person-of-the-forest

In the Indonesian language, the meaning of orang *is person, while* hutan *means forest. Orang-utans have inspired many myths. One is that orang-utans were once humans exiled to the trees for displeasing the gods. Another is that they are descended from a man who ran away into the forest because he owed money.*

Food and Feeding

▲ HUNGRY GIBBON

Gibbons are mainly frugivores (feeding on fruit) but they also eat leaves and occasionally insects and eggs. They are so light that they can hang from thin branches and reach out their long arms to pick fruit growing right at the ends. Gibbons eat mainly ripe fruit.

FRUIT-EATERS ▶

Fruit forms about 65 per cent of an orang-utan's diet. The apes spread the seeds of fruit trees over a wide area by passing the seeds in their droppings far from the parent tree. This female has found a bunch of bananas but another favourite food of the orangutan is durian tree fruit. The football-sized fruit contains a sweet-tasting but foul-smelling flesh, which they adore. Orang-utans also eat leaves, shoots, insects and eggs.

Apes feed mainly on fruit and leaves, but they also eat a small amount of animal food, such as insects. Chimpanzees have a more varied diet than the other apes and occasionally eat red meat from birds and mammals, such as monkeys and young antelopes. Orang-utans have also been seen eating young birds and squirrels. Apes spend a lot of time travelling around to find their food, which is spread out through the forest. If they stayed in one place, they would quickly use up all the food. They remember the locations of the best fruit trees in their area, and know when they will bear fruit. Apes have to eat a lot of food because their mainly plant food diet is often low in nutrients. As they cannot digest the tough fibres (cellulose) in the stems and leaves, much of what they eat passes through their gut undigested and out in their dung.

▲ MASSIVE MEALS

Gorillas are mainly herbivores, munching their way through 20–30kg of greens every day. They eat with a lot of lip smacking and other noises of appreciation. Gorillas are careful eaters, often preparing their food by folding leaves into a wodge or peeling off inedible layers. They drop any unwanted bits, such as stalks, in a neat pile.

▲ HUNTING CHIMPS

Chimpanzees are clever predators, occasionally banding together in small groups to chase and catch animals such as monkeys, small antelopes and bush pigs. A hunt can be long, lasting up to two hours, involving high-speed chases and ambushes, and causing great excitement.

▼ CHIMP MEALS

Chimpanzees spend about six hours a day feeding, mostly just after sunrise and just before sunset. They eat a lot of fruit, which makes up about 68 per cent of their diet, but they also eat leaves and other plant matter, as well as meat and insects.

▲ FOOD ALL AROUND

Mountain gorillas don't have to look very hard to find something to eat. Their plant food is all around them, so they just have to reach out a hand to pick a meal. Since they need to eat a lot of food, meals last two to four hours at a time. Gorilla days are mainly spent walking and eating food, then resting between meals to digest it. Their big stomach stores the food while it is being digested.

chimpanzee
(Pan troglodytes)

27

Ape Senses

Apes are creatures of the daytime and their most important sense is their keen eyesight. Their forward-facing eyes can pick up fine detail, judge distances and see in colour. Their nose is a small, but useful, back-up to the eyes. Their sense of smell is probably better than that of humans. Apes sniff food and each other and also use their sense of smell to warn them of something unusual in their environment. If they do not recognize a smell, or if it makes them uneasy, they will use their eyes to investigate. The fact that apes rely more on sight than smell may be one reason why they have little hair on their faces. Facial expressions are easier to see without hair getting in the way, so they can be used as visual signals for communication.

▲ **EXCELLENT EYES**
The eyes of apes are set close together, facing forwards. This enables both eyes to focus on the same object. The overlapping fields of vision allow three-dimensional sight for judging distance and depth accurately. This helps them to jump from branch to branch without falling.

◄ **NOSEPRINTS** ►
Individual gorillas can be identified by the shape of their noses. The folds, wrinkles and outline of a gorilla's nose are just as distinctive as its fingerprint. Each of the three subspecies of gorilla also has a different nose shape. These differences are especially clear when the nose of the mountain gorilla (left) is compared with that of a western lowland gorilla (right).

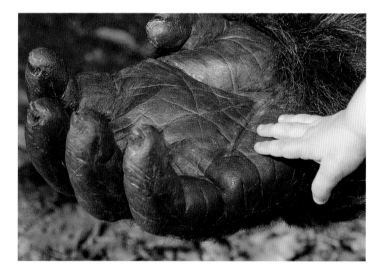

▲ SENSITIVE SKIN

Like humans, gorillas have tiny raised ridges, or fingerprints, on the tips of their fingers. These ridges help gorillas feel and hold on to objects. Each gorilla's fingerprint is unique. Flat nails protect the sensitive fingertips from damage. A gorilla's hands respond to temperature and pressure as well as to touch.

Did you know? Male orang-utans use a long call to attract females and to keep other males away.

Three Wise Monkeys

A set of three Japanese monkeys were once used to explain Buddhist teachings. One monkey is covering its ears – this one represents the idea of hear no evil. Another has its hands over its eyes so that it can see no evil. The third is stopping words from coming out of its mouth – representing the third wise saying of speak no evil.

NOISY APE ▶

Gibbons greatly rely on sound for communicating among the leafy treetops. When the siamang sings, its throat pouch swells up with air. This pouch of air acts like a resonating chamber to make its song even louder. Some other gibbons have these pouches too, but not such big ones.

▼ SOUND SENSE

Big ears help chimpanzees to pick up the sounds drifting through the forest. They often stop and listen for the sounds of chimps or other animals, which may tell them of approaching danger. They also hoot to each other to keep in contact.

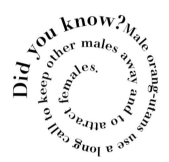

Smart Apes

Apes appear to be the brightest of all the non-human animals, but it is difficult to measure intelligence. Scientists think an intelligent animal is one that can solve problems, investigate and adapt to new conditions, behave in a flexible way, remember things, use tools, pass on information from one generation to the next and even use language. Apes can do all these things, although their throats cannot make the sounds used by humans to produce a spoken language. Scientists have experimented with teaching apes signs and symbols in order to understand them better and to investigate their intelligence. There is much debate about whether chimpanzees, bonobos, gorillas or orang-utans are the most intelligent of the great apes.

▲ **ESCAPE ARTISTS**
Captive orang-utans are the master escapologists of the ape world. They use branches to ford deep moats full of water around their enclosures. They take out the centre pins from hinges to open doors the wrong way, and they unravel chain link fences.

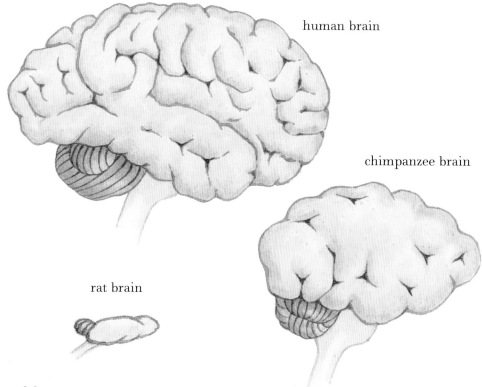

human brain

chimpanzee brain

rat brain

◄ **BRAIN POWER**
Humans and chimpanzees have much bigger brains than rats, even compared to body size. The bigger the brain, the less tied an animal is to fixed ways of doing things. Humans and chimps have large areas of the brain for learning, memory, reasoning and judgement. This helps them to make decisions about what to do next, where to go and what to eat.

30

▲ COMPUTER APE

At the Yerkes Regional Primate Center in Georgia, USA, bonobos and chimpanzees have been taught to communicate with a computer.

◀ APE ART

Many people have suggested that the way humans use art to express ideas is a measure of our intelligence. When captive apes have been allowed to experiment with pencils, paints and paper, they have produced a variety of interesting images.

▲ HAND SPEAK

All four great apes have been taught sign language for simple communication. The apes have even taught fellow apes. Bonobos, such as Kanzi (above), have learned to communicate by pointing to specific symbols on a large board.

Planet of the Apes

In the film Planet of the Apes *(1968), three astronauts find themselves on a planet where apes are in control. Orang-utans are judges, chimpanzees are scholars and gorillas are police. Humans are hunted as stupid beasts. The hero realizes that this is an Earth of the future, where ape and human roles are reversed.*

Focus on

Humans were once thought to be the only animals clever enough to use tools. Now we know that a handful of other animals, such as Galapagos finches and sea otters, use them too. However, these animals are only beginners compared to chimpanzees. A chimp chooses its tools, changes them to make them better and uses them over and over again. Chimps plan ahead, collecting sticks or stones on their way to a source of food. Their nimble fingers and creative minds help them to invent and use tools. Adult chimps are good at concentrating, sometimes spending hours using their tools.

USING A STICK
This chimpanzee is shaping a stick to help her dig for food. Chimpanzees have invented clever ways to use sticks.

TASTY SNACKS
An intelligent chimp can shape and manipulate a grass stem to form a useful tool for fishing out termites from a mound. Scientists who have tried to copy the chimps have found that termite fishing is much, much harder than it looks.

SWEET AS HONEY
A captive chimp is using a stick, in the same way as a chimp in the wild would use a grass stem, to fish in a termite mound. However, the termite mound in the zoo probably has yogurt or honey inside it, rather than termites.

Chimp Tools

LEAF SPONGE

A wodge of leaves makes a useful sponge to soak up rainwater from tree holes. Chewing the leaf first breaks up its waterproof coating, so it soaks up more water. Leaves may also be used as toilet paper, to wipe blood from wounds and to scrape up sticky food.

STICK TOOLS

Wild chimps can only make tools from objects in their environment, which is why sticks are so important. Sticks make good weapons for attack and defence. They can also be used as levers, and thin sticks make a natural dental floss.

NUTCRACKERS

In West Africa, chimps use hammers and anvils to crack open the hard shells of nuts. Hammers are made from logs or stones, anvils from stones or tree roots. Hammer stones can weigh as much as 20kg. A skilled adult can crack a shell with just a few blows.

Living in a Group

▲ **GENTLE GIANTS**

Life in a gorilla group is generally peaceful and friendly and there is seldom serious fighting within the group. The silverback can stop most squabbles by strutting and glaring at the troublemakers. He is the group's leader, deciding where it will travel and when it will settle.

Of all the apes, chimpanzees live in the largest groups – up to about 100 individuals. The chimps constantly change their friends and often drop out altogether to spend time on their own. A chimpanzee group is based around the most important male chimps, like gorilla groups, where one of the male silverbacks leads his group. Bonobos live in smaller groups than chimpanzees, but their society is led by females rather than males. Orang-utans tend to live on their own, although females and their young spend a lot of time together while the youngster is growing up. Gibbons have a completely different social system from that of the other apes – they live in family groups of a mother, father and their young.

Did you know? A silverback male is prepared to die to defend his group.

bonobos
(*Pan paniscus*)

▼ **SOCIABLE SOCIETY**

Bonobos are very sociable creatures. Most of the time they live in large, loose groups, called communities, which are split up into smaller groups of 15 or less when foraging for food.

juvenile male

male silverback leader

adult female

young gorilla

◄ **HAPPY FAMILIES**
Gorillas like to live in extended family groups, usually with between five and thirty members. A gorilla without a group will do its best to join one or start a new one. Each group is controlled and defended by a large adult silverback male.

▲ **TREETOP FAMILIES**
Gibbons are the only apes to live in pairs and mate for life. They may have two or three young with them, as they do not leave their parents until they are six or seven years old. The interval between births is two-and-a-half to three years.

LONE ORANG ▶
Orang-utans spend most of their time alone. One reason for this may be that they need to eat a lot of fruit every day. If lots of orang-utans lived together, they would not be able to find enough fruit to eat. Even when they do meet, they often ignore each other.

GIRL POWER ▶
Females form the backbone of a bonobo group. Adult female bonobos form strong friendships, which are reinforced by grooming and hugging each other. This group of female bonobos have been raised in captivity. Boredom in captivity leads some apes to pluck out their hair.

bonobos
(Pan paniscus)

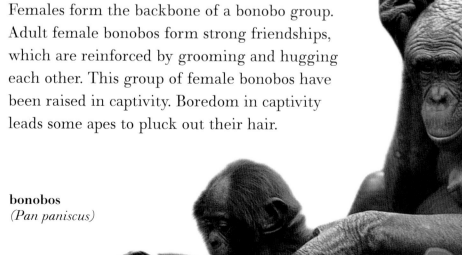

Communication

▼ **GIBBON DUET**
Many pairs of adult gibbons sing to warn other gibbons to stay out of their territories. The duet may also help the pair to stay together. Singing gibbons fill the forest with a chorus of noisy whoops, hoots and wails.

Although apes cannot speak, they communicate with a variety of sounds, facial expressions and gestures. Scientists have even learned some of this ape-speak in order to reassure the apes they are studying, and avoid frightening the animals away. Orang-utans and gibbons both call loudly to stake their claim to their territory, rather as we would put up a fence and a 'keep out' sign around our property. In chimp and gorilla societies, body positions and gestures show which animals are most important, or dominant, and which are least important, or submissive. Chimps and gorillas also communicate through a variety of sounds, especially chimps, who can be very noisy apes.

▲ **PULLING FACES**
Chimpanzees have a variety of different expressions for communication. A wide, open and relaxed mouth is a play face used to start, or during, a game. An angry chimp clenches his lips shut.

siamang gibbon
(Hylobates syndactylus)

◀ A GAME OF BLUFF

Rising on his back legs, a male silverback gorilla slaps his cupped hands rapidly against his chest, making a 'pok-pok-pok' sound. Then he charges forwards, tearing up plants and slapping the ground. This display is really a bluff to scare away rivals. Gorillas hardly ever fight, and a male usually stops his charge at the last minute.

▲ GORILLA-SPEAK

Researchers observing gorillas in the wild have learned to make the same sounds and gestures as the gorillas. A content gorilla makes a rumbling belch sound. A sharp, pig-grunt noise means the gorilla is annoyed.

◀ KEEP OUT!

Fully grown male orang-utans usually keep to their own area of forest — up to 10 sq km. This is called their home range. Every day, a male roars loudly to warn other orang-utans to stay away. This long call lasts for about two minutes. By calling, males avoid meetings that might end in a fight.

TOP CHIMP ▶

The dominant chimpanzee in a group shows off occasionally by charging about screaming and throwing branches. He also hunches his shoulders and makes his hair stand up on end.

▼ LOW RANK

To avoid fighting with important chimps, low-ranking chimps behave in a certain way. They flatten their hair, crouch down or bob up and down, and back towards the more important chimp, while pant-grunting.

Focus on

All the chimpanzees in a community know each other well. Mothers have a very strong bond with their young, and many chimps who are not related form close friendships, especially males. Dominant males form the stable core of a chimpanzee group and they will attack and even kill males from other communities. Female chimps may emigrate to a neighbouring community. Members of a community will meet, spend time together and then separate throughout the day. In chimp society there is a hierarchy of importance, which is maintained by powerful males. The chimps jostle for position, constantly checking where they stand with each other and challenging their leaders.

YOU GROOM MY BACK

One of the most important activities in a chimpanzee group is grooming. It helps to keep the group together by allowing the chimps to strengthen friendships and patch up quarrels. High-ranking chimps are often groomed by low-ranking ones. It takes a young chimp about two years to learn how to groom properly.

MOTHERS AND BABIES

Rank is not inherited in chimpanzee society, so a young chimp with a high-ranking mother will not necessarily be important itself. But high-ranking mothers are more secure and confident, showing by their behaviour how to become a high-ranking chimp. Female chimps become more important in a group as they get older and have more young.

the Chimp Group

GANG WARFARE
A dominant male chimp often makes friends with two or three others, who spend their time with him and back him up in fights. Powerful supporters enable a chimp to become a leader.

PLAYTIME
As young chimpanzees play, they get to know how to mix with the other chimps in a group. They learn how to greet others and which individuals are the most important.

FRIENDSHIP
To show their affection for one another, chimps hug, kiss and pat each other on the back. As males spend much more time together than females, this friendly contact is more common between males, although females strike up special friendships, too.

NOISY CHIMPS
Chimpanzees make more than 30 different sounds. When they are contented, they make soft 'hooing' noises, when they discover food they hoot, and they scream when excited.

Defence

The great apes are too big to be killed and eaten by most animals. Sometimes a tiger, leopard, snake or crocodile does succeed in catching an ape, although they probably pick on the old, the young and the sick. Apes can also be injured or even killed in battles with members of their own species. But their main enemy is people, who destroy their habitat, kill them for meat or capture them as pets or for medical research. Living in a group is a good defence, as members can warn each other of danger and help to defend each other. Apes that live in smaller groups or on their own, such as gibbons and orang-utans, can escape danger by living high in the trees.

▲ **SILVER PROTECTION**
If a leopard or similar predator threatens a group of gorillas, the silverback leader puts himself between his family and the danger. The females and youngsters in the group huddle together and rely on the silverback to drive away the intruder.

◄ **FRIEND OR FOE?**
This frightened chimpanzee is seeking reassurance by holding out her hand. When they are faced with human predators, chimps usually keep quiet and still or melt away into the bush, but they will attack leopards with long branches and big stones. A chimp's sharp teeth can also inflict a nasty bite.

◄ HUNTED
Leopards are clever hunters, and especially dangerous because they hunt at night. Their spotted coats camouflage them well and they are excellent tree climbers. Leopards are very agile in trees, so they can spring on apes from overhead.

leopard
(Panthera pardus)

▲ ILLEGAL KILLERS
Apes are protected by law, but poachers (illegal hunters) break the rules because they hope to make money. Here, a pair of gorillas were shot so that their infant could be captured and sold.

▲ CONFUSING GRIN
This chimpanzee may look as if it is smiling, but in fact it is showing its teeth and gums in a fear grin. Chimps make this sort of face when they are frightened or nervous.

Killer Orang-utan
In 1841, the American writer Edgar Allen Poe published his story The Murders in the Rue Morgue. *In a mysterious and macabre tale, Poe describes how an orang-utan escapes from its cage and finds shelter in the home of Madame L'Espanaye and her daughter. Terrified by the two women's cries of fear, the orang-utan seizes a razor and cuts their throats.*

41

Courtship

Ape courtship involves choosing, attracting and mating with a partner. Apes breed at any time of year and have various courtship patterns, using sounds, scents and displays to attract a mate. Chimps and bonobos use mating as a form of communication within their groups. It helps to relieve tension and keep the group together. Females in season accept many different mates and they mate quickly and often. Mating is less frequent in gorillas and gibbons. They mate mainly to reproduce but the act lasts somewhat longer. Usually, one male gorilla mates with all the females in his group. Male gibbons usually have just one mate, but some do father other infants. Orang-utans pair mainly for courtship and mating, but Sumatran orang-utans may stay together for two or three weeks so that the male can protect the pregnant female. Mating lasts much longer and is more varied in orang-utans than in other apes.

▲ **ORANG-UTAN COURTING**
These young orang-utans are practising their courtship behaviour for when they grow up. Courtship in orang-utans can last for less than an hour – or stretch to fill many weeks.

◄ **IN THE PINK**
When a female chimpanzee is ready to mate, she develops a pinkish swelling on her rear end that sticks out like a pink balloon full of water. This happens every four weeks or so. The female's pink bottom attracts the attention of every nearby male chimp.

chimpanzee
(Pan troglodytes)

▲ GIBBON PAIRS

Young male gibbons often sing to attract a female, but they also wander away from their parents in search of a mate. Once a male gibbon finds a mate, he stays with her for life. One of the most characteristic sounds of the Asian forests are the loud, spectacular calls of dueting gibbons echoing through the trees.

▲ PRETEND PLAY

These young gorillas are practising their fighting skills as they play together. When they grow up and lead their own group, these skills will help them to protect a secure area for the group to live in. Then they will be able to court and mate with the females in their group.

▲ GORILLA MATES

The weather and food supply in a gorilla's habitat are similar all year round, so gorillas mate and give birth at any time of year. Females may ask a male to mate by backing up to the male with their rear end in the air and their elbows on the ground.

▲ HANGING HAIR

Male Sumatran orang-utans sometimes display their beautful orange hair to females by hanging down from branches. This helps a female to decide if he has the strength to protect her from other males.

43

Focus on

Bonobos live a very peaceful lifestyle and are affectionate and gentle apes. They seem to have adopted a make-love-not-war attitude to life. Sexual behaviour is an important part of their everyday life, even when they are youngsters. It is used not only for reproduction and having babies but also as a way of getting on with other members of the group. Females will mate at any time, and with lots of different males, which helps to calm the group down and avoid conflict. Both male and female bonobos also carry out sexually related behaviour with others of the same gender. These activities help to constantly reassure the bonobos and keep the group close together.

MALE ROLES

Bonobo males have less status than females, so they do not dominate their groups. Unlike male chimps, male bonobos do not form strong friendships. Instead, they remain close to their mother.

FEMALE IMPORTANCE

The females form the backbone of bonobo groups. Female bonobos may use mating as a way of persuading males to give them food. Low-ranking females seem to mate more than high-ranking ones. This may help them to cope with their less important status in the group, and make the group as a whole more peaceful.

Bonobos

MATING ADVERT
Their pink bottoms make it very obvious when female bonobos are ready to mate. These mating adverts last much longer in bonobos than in chimpanzees.

TENDER TOUCH
Bonobos often touch each other, mate or groom each other to calm themselves down at a time of excitement or tension. They travel in smaller groups than chimpanzees. Often, a male, a female and the female's young will form a group. Bonobo groups also do not change as much as chimpanzee groups.

BRIEF MATING
Mating in bonobos is a low-key affair, and at least a quarter of all bonobo matings are started by the female. The act of mating lasts only about 15 seconds.

FACE-TO-FACE
Bonobos are unusual among the apes in that they sometimes mate face-to-face, although gorillas, orangutans and gibbons occasionally do this too. Mating can be used as a greeting or take place at times of great excitement, such as when a supply of favourite food has been found.

45

Birth and Babies

Like humans, apes usually have one baby at a time and spend many years looking after their young. In chimps, bonobos, gorillas and orangutans, the baby develops for about eight or nine months inside its mother before being born. Baby gibbons are born after a development of only seven or eight months. Baby apes are much smaller than human babies and weigh only about half as much. This means it is much easier for a mother ape to give birth than for a human mother. Both labour and birth are fairly swift and trouble-free.

Newborn apes are helpless, but they have a very strong grip to cling to their mother's hair. She feeds them on her milk and carries them around for four or five years as they gradually grow up and become independent.

▲ **NEWBORN GORILLA**
This day-old gorilla is tiny and helpless. Its wrinkled face is a pinkish colour, its big ears stick out and it has very little hair. Soon after birth, the baby's brown eyes open and peer curiously at its surroundings. Despite its long, skinny arms and legs, the baby gorilla is quite strong.

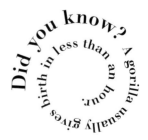
Did you know? A gorilla usually gives birth in less than an hour.

◄ **MILK BAR**
A newborn baby gorilla depends on its mother's milk for nourishment. After six to eight months, it gradually begins to try different bits of plant food, but it will continue to drink its mother's milk for at least two years.

PIGGY-BACK ▶

Riding piggy-back on its mother's broad back, a baby gorilla watches the other gorillas and looks around its habitat as the group travels from place to place. This is the safest place for the young gorilla until it is strong enough to walk by itself. A young gorilla cannot do this until it is at least two-and-a-half or three years old.

▲ HITCHING A RIDE

Very young baby chimps are carried underneath their mother, clinging on to her fur with their tiny fists. By the age of five to six months, a baby chimp starts to ride on its mother's back. It is alert, looking around and touching things.

◄ TREETOP BABIES

Baby gibbons depend on their mothers for warmth and milk. Gibbon fathers groom their babies and play with them. Siamang gibbon fathers look after their youngsters during the day.

▲ CHIMP CHILDHOOD

The bond between a mother chimpanzee and her baby is strong and lasts throughout their lives. A young chimp is completely dependent on its mother for the first five years of its life, staying where its mother can see or hear it.

Focus on Young

MOTHER LOVE

There is a very strong bond between a mother orang-utan and her baby. When she is not moving through the trees or feeding, the mother may groom her baby or suckle it, but she doesn't often play with it. A baby orang-utan may scream and throw a tantrum to get its mother's attention.

A young orang-utan grows up in a world almost entirely filled by its mother, and for the first year of its life, is entirely dependent on her. Following the birth of a baby, a mother orang-utan becomes even more shy than usual. She tries to avoid other animals in order to protect her baby. The solitary life of a young orang-utan is very different from that of a young chimp, bonobo or gorilla, since they have other youngsters to play with and other adults to help care for them. A young orang-utan stays with its mother for seven to nine years, gradually learning what to eat, where to find food, how to climb and swing through the trees safely, and how to make a nest to sleep in.

MOTHER'S MILK

For the first year of its life, a baby orang-utan drinks its mother's milk and clings to her chest or back. After a year, it starts to eat solid food but it continues to suck for another three to five years. Like most baby mammals, orang-utans are keen to take their mother's milk for as long as possible.

Orang-utans

NEST-BUILDING

Baby orang-utans share their mother's nest at night. During their second year, they start to experiment with making their own nests.

PLAYTIME

Although they are usually solitary, on the rare occasions young orang-utans meet, they wrestle and play together in the forest. They may get so carried away that they do not notice when their mother leaves. Then they have to hurry after her, screaming angrily as they go.

SOLID FOOD

To start her baby on solid food, a mother orang-utan partly chews up bits of food and then presses them into the baby's mouth. Young orang-utans eagerly take the solid food.

A NEW BABY

When an orang-utan is between five and eight years old, its mother may give birth again. The new baby takes the mother's attention and the young orang-utan becomes more independent. It may stay with its mother for a year or more after a new baby is born.

Growing Up

Apes spend a long time growing up. As well as learning how to move, feed and defend themselves, they have to know how to behave with others of their own kind. This is especially important for chimpanzees and gorillas because they live in large groups. Young apes do not become independent of their mothers until they are about eight years old. Female orang-utans and gorillas may have babies at about ten years of age, but chimps do not have babies until they are about 14 years old. Male gorillas and orang-utans mature later than females, at about 15 years old. When they are grown-up, orang-utans and gibbons leave their parents to start a life of their own. Most gorillas and female chimps also leave the group they were born into.

orang-utans
(Pongo pygmaeus)

▲ **MOTHER AND BABY**
Female orang-utans spend most of their adult lives caring for their offspring. An orang-utan may have only four young in her lifetime.

▲ **APE EXPLORER**
Chimpanzees love to explore, moving further away from their mothers as they test out their climbing skills. At the first sign of danger, they run back to their mother.

▲ SPEEDY GORILLAS

Young gorillas develop through the same stages of movement as human babies, only much faster. They can crawl at nine weeks of age and walk between five to eight months – a stage when most human babies haven't started to crawl.

◄ PLAYING THE GAME

The little chimps have a lot of free time, which they spend at play. Young females spend much of their time playing with the babies in their group. Through playing, the chimps learn the rules of chimpanzee society.

chimpanzee
(Pan troglodytes)

Did you know? Young gorillas have a white tail tuft to help their mother's find them.

▲ FOOD FROM MOTHER

A chimpanzee watches its mother and other chimps to find out what is good to eat. Young chimps chew the other end of whatever food their mother is eating.

► AT PLAY

Young gorillas wrestle, chase, play-fight and climb and slide all over the adults. This helps them to test their strength, build up their muscles and learn how to get along with other gorillas.

Orphan Apes

▲ GORILLA ORPHANAGE

Congolese conservationist Dr Ndinga Assitou holds an orphan gorilla at the Brazzaville Gorilla Orphanage. Sick and wounded little gorillas that have been confiscated from poachers and illegal traders recover and grow up at this orphanage before being returned to the wild.

Sometimes, mother apes are killed by disease, or they die of old age or natural causes, leaving their babies as orphans. Poachers may also kill mothers for meat or to capture their babies. In a zoo, a mother ape may not be able to care for her baby. All these orphans find life very difficult. They no longer have the comfort of being with their mother and feeling safe under her protection. They cannot watch their mother to learn what to eat and how to behave. People have tried to care for some of these orphan apes, teaching them how to survive in the wild and releasing them when they can look after themselves. It takes time for orphans to adapt to life in the wild. They cannot survive if they have to compete with wild apes. Many orphan apes are cared for in special sanctuaries where they have more freedom than in a zoo.

BOTTLED MILK ▶

The milk of a mother ape contains a balanced mixture of food to help babies grow fit and strong. Orphan apes are fed on powdered milk, which they drink from bottles. This is not as good for them as their mother's milk, nor do they get the comfort of being held close to their mother's body while they feed.

▲ A NEW LIFE

Baby orang-utans were popular as pets in Asia, and poachers still shoot mothers to sell their babies as pets. However, it is illegal to own a pet orang-utan. Some of these orphans are taken away from their owners and sent to special centres where they can be cared for and prepared for a possible life in the wild.

▲ LONELY CHIMP

Baby chimps are very close to their mothers. This emotional bond is so strong that when a mother dies, her infant often dies too. Wild orphans have a better chance of survival if cared for by older sisters and brothers.

western lowland gorilla
(Gorilla gorilla gorilla)

◄ ZOO APES

Zoos try to leave young apes with their mothers. However, if the mother does not know how to look after her infant, or if it is sickly, then a keeper has to care for it. Apes that have grown up with keepers, instead of their mothers, tend to behave differently.

▲ HUMAN APES

When apes have lived with humans for a long time, it is difficult for them to get along with other apes of their species. They behave in a different way from wild apes and they are dependent on people for food. They can only be released back into the wild if a suitably safe habitat can be found and food provided.

53

Ape Ancestors

The first apes appeared on Earth some 20 million years ago, but their early evolution is difficult to trace accurately because few of their fossils (preserved remains) have been discovered. Early apes were heavier than monkeys, swinging underneath branches and using their powerful arms for support. Some of these early apes died out, leaving just six groups to evolve through to the present day. Scientific tests suggest that chimpanzees and humans separated between six and eight million years ago and went on to develop in their own ways. Gorillas branched out earlier, possibly six to nine million years ago; orang-utans 12–16 million years ago and gibbons 20 million years ago. However, there is great debate about these dates.

▲ HANDY MAN

This is a model of *Homo habilis*, or handy man, an early human named after its ability to make simple stone tools. *Homo habilis* lived about two million years ago in Africa and was about 1.3m tall. Although their brains were only half the size of modern-day humans, they could probably speak.

FOSSIL APES ▼

Apes probably evolved from a group known as *Aegyptopithecus* (Egyptian ape), which lived in North Africa some 30 million years ago. Other fossil apes include *Dryopithecus* or woodland ape (about 18 million years ago), *Ramapithecus* (eight–fifteen million years ago) and *Gigantopithecus* (six–nine million years ago). The *Gigantopithecus* apes died out, but *Dryopithecus* and *Ramapithecus* evolved into modern apes, including humans.

Aegyptopithecus

Dryopithecus

Gigantopithecus

chimp bonobo human gorilla orangutan lesser apes monkey

0

5

10

15

Millions of years ago

20

25

30

35

Did you know? *Apes were more common than monkeys 20 million years ago. Today the reverse is true.*

◄ FAMILY TREE

There is a lot of debate about the evolution of the apes. This is just one family tree showing possible dates and pathways taken by the different apes as they evolved over some 20 million years. The human and ape lines of evolution may have separated about five to seven million years ago. Monkeys evolved earlier than apes, about 30 million years ago.

◄ APE THEORY

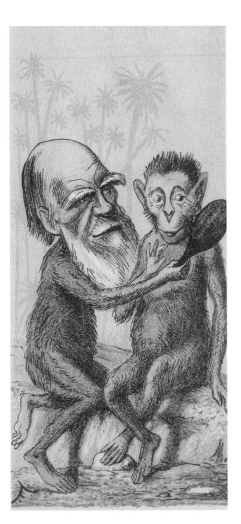

In 1871, Charles Darwin published a book called *The Descent of Man* in which he suggested that humans had evolved from ape-like ancestors. Many people were shocked by this idea and made fun of Darwin in cartoons such as this one. What Darwin meant was that people and apes evolved along separate lines from earlier, ape-like animals.

▼ A COMMON ANCESTOR?

Some scientists have suggested that a small tree-climbing animal, similar to modern tree shrews, may have been the ancestor of all primates, such as lemurs, monkeys, apes and humans. However, recent evidence suggests that they might not be so closely related.

treeshrew *(Tupaia lyonogale tana)*

Primitive Primates

Lemurs, bush babies, lorises, pottos and tarsiers are all known as primitive primates or prosimians, meaning pre-monkeys. The other main group of primates – sometimes called the higher primates – includes marmosets and tamarins, monkeys, apes and humans. Prosimians are different from monkeys, apes and humans because they have smaller brains and a far better sense of smell. They also tend to have longer, dog-like snouts, while monkeys (except for baboons), apes and humans have more rounded heads. One of the most distinctive groups of prosimians is the lemurs of Madagascar. The name lemur means ghost and refers to their mysterious life in the trees. Early primates may have looked rather like modern lemurs and followed a similar lifestyle.

▲ LEAPING LEGS

A bush baby's back legs can be twice as long as its body. These extraordinarily long legs allow a bush baby to make huge leaps through the rainforest branches. Its large, forward-seeing eyes help it judge the space between branches so it lands safely.

STRIPY TAILS ▶

Ring-tailed lemurs live in groups with up to 30 members. The striped tail is longer than the total length of the head and body. It is used for signalling messages to other lemurs, and can also be rubbed with scent to send smelly messages. The sense of smell is more important in lemurs than in apes.

ring-tailed lemurs
(Lemur catta)

56

FINGER FOOD ▶

The most extraordinary part of an aye-aye's body is its long, spindly middle finger. It uses this to winkle out wood-boring insects from tree trunks, and scoop the insides out of hard-shelled fruits. Unlike other primates, the aye-aye has claws on the ends of its fingers and most toes.

◀ STILL AS STATUES

The potto lives among thick rainforest vegetation and moves so slowly and carefully that it is very hard to see. At the slightest sign of danger, the potto freezes completely still. It can stay like this for hours. Its grasping feet and hands give it a strong grip on branches.

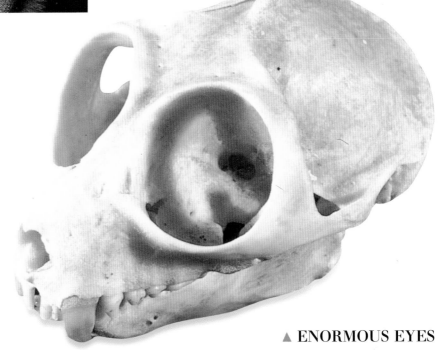

▲ TWIN TAXI

This silvery marmoset is the father of the two babies on his back. Father marmosets are very involved in bringing up babies — which is hard work because marmosets usually have twins.

▲ ENORMOUS EYES

The most obvious feature of a loris's skull is its huge eye sockets, which are protected by a thick, bony ridge. A loris is active at night and needs its huge eyes to help it to see in the dark. Lorises also have a well-developed sense of smell, and a face covered with hair.

57

Working Primates

People have often used monkeys and apes for entertainment, to help them carry out tasks, or for scientific experiments. Nowadays, it is illegal to export apes from the wild. Captured apes may be well looked after, but often they are kept in very bad conditions and do not live long. They may even die on the journey from their natural habitat, especially if they are transported in cramped containers with no food or water. Even when they do survive, captured apes or monkeys live a very artificial life, away from their natural homes and families. Some of them may suffer a lot of pain during scientific experiments. In an ideal world, we would stop using apes or monkeys for our own ends. We should certainly prevent the use of such intelligent creatures simply as playthings and curiosities.

▲ **APE ADVERTS**
Chimpanzees are sometimes dressed up in human clothes and used in advertisements. While some people can make a lot of money, others believe it is wrong to use apes in this way.

◄ **TRIED AND TESTED**
Many chimps have been used for medical research because they are so similar to humans. Gorillas and orang-utans are too big to keep and handle easily. In the 1960s and 1970s chimps were forced to smoke cigarettes to test for lung diseases. They were also used for brain experiments. Today, such harmful and inhuman experiments are less common, but some are still tested with diseases in some countries.

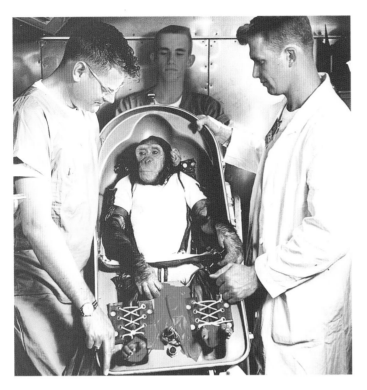

▲ SPACE APE

In 1961, a chimp was the first live creature to be sent into space by the USA. He was monitored throughout the flight by cameras. This flight paved the way for the first human voyages into space, but we can only guess at how the chimp felt about such a terrifying experience.

▲ HELPING HAND

In Thailand, pig-tailed macaques are trained to collect coconuts for their owners in return for food rewards. The macaques are much better than people at climbing trees.

◀ BEACH CHIMPS

Visitors to popular beaches in the Mediterranean may have their photo taken with a young chimpanzee. They do not realize that many of these chimps are illegal and ill-treated by their owners. Most die of neglect within a year or so. The use of beach chimps has been banned in many areas, but not wiped out completely.

▲ MOVIE STAR

A female orang-utan starred alongside Clint Eastwood in the movie *Every Which Way But Loose* (1978) and in the sequel *Any Which Way You Can.* The plot featured the travels of a prize fighter and Clyde, the orang-utan.

PEOPLE AND APES

Apes in Danger

Apes live in a steadily shrinking habitat. Their forest and woodland homes have been gradually replaced by farms, grazing lands and villages. Vast areas of rainforest have been flooded by the water held back by dams, and other areas have been dug up by mining companies looking for precious minerals and metals. Even when apes live in protected areas, they are still illegally hunted for their meat or body parts, or captured to be sold as pets or for medical research. In times of war, apes are further threatened by land mines and the movement of large numbers of refugees into their habitat. People can also pass on diseases to apes, often without realizing that they have done so.

▲ **POACHING**

This is some of the kit used by poachers to kill apes and antelopes illegally in protected areas such as national parks. Wire snares concealed in the undergrowth can prove deadly to apes trapped in their tight grip. Traditional hunting weapons such as spears and arrows may also be used.

Did you know? There are just 630 mountain gorillas in the world.

APE BODIES ▶

Ape body parts are sometimes sold as grisly souvenirs. These gorilla skulls are for sale on a traditional African medicine stall where they are used as fetishes (a type of good luck charm). There would be no reason for poachers to kill apes if people were not prepared to buy their body parts. Gorillas are also killed for meat. Some of it feeds workers cutting down the forests. The rest is sold in city markets.

60

▲ FOREST DESTRUCTION

The greatest danger to all apes and monkeys is the destruction of their habitat, especially the rainforests. An area of rainforest the size of four football pitches disappears every minute. Rainforests are destroyed for their valuable timber, or to make way for cattle ranches or plantations of cash crops.

▲ THREAT OF WAR

In the mid 1990s, civil war and genocide in Rwanda led thousands of people to raid the national park of the mountain gorillas for firewood and food.

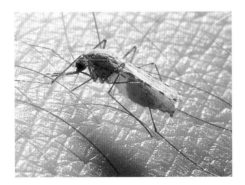

▲ DISEASES

Since apes are so similar to us, they suffer from many of the same diseases. For example, apes can catch malaria, carried by mosquitoes.

FOREST FIRES ▶

In the late 1990s, forest fires raged across Borneo and Sumatra, killing many orang-utans, destroying their habitat and causing breathing problems for the survivors.

Conservation

Gorillas, orang-utans, chimpanzees and bonobos are now officially recognized as endangered species. Laws have been passed to stop live apes and parts of their bodies being bought or sold. However, laws can never give total protection to wild animals, especially when people can make a lot of money by breaking the law. To help apes survive in the future, their habitat needs to be protected in national parks or reserves. Apes bred in captivity might one day be released into the wild but only if suitable natural habitats can be found. Conserving apes takes a lot of time and costs a lot of money. Many of the countries where the apes live have very little money and need help for conservation from richer nations. Apes are more like humans than any other animal. It will be tragic if we cannot find a way to share our future with them.

▲ GORILLAS IN THE MIST
Dian Fossey wrote about her work with mountain gorillas in *Gorillas in the Mist*, later made into a film starring Sigourney Weaver (above). The film raised awareness of the gorilla's plight.

▼ HABITAT ZOOS
Some good zoos now keep apes in large, tree-filled enclosures, which are as much like their natural habitat as possible. Breeding apes in zoos helps to increase their numbers.

western lowland gorillas
(*Gorilla gorilla gorilla*)

▲ TOURIST DOLLARS

Many people pay a lot of money to get close to a wild great ape, but this is too close as the ape could catch human flu. If tourists are carefully controlled, they provide money to pay for conservation.

▼ POACHING PATROL

These wardens are patrolling the national park where the mountain gorillas live. They are keeping a sharp lookout for armed poachers and their snares. If there is a shoot-out, both the wardens and the poachers may be killed.

◀ CHIMFUNSHI ORPHANAGE

David and Sheila Siddle have converted their farm in Zambia into the Chimfunshi Wildlife Orphanage to look after rescued chimps from the Congo. The Siddles have walled and fenced off their land and allow the chimps to climb trees, build nests and live like wild chimpanzees.

▶ EDGE OF SURVIVAL

In developing countries where most families grow their own food, there is an increasing need for more land. Forests are cleared right up to the park boundary, as can be seen in this photograph, which shows the edge of the Virunga National Park in the Congo. If gorillas and elephants wander out searching for food, they are labelled 'crop raiders' by local farmers, who are desperate to protect their only source of food or income.

THE WORLD OF MONKEYS

Monkeys are a more varied group of animals than their popular image suggests. Not all are cheeky, scampering animals that chatter at you from the branches. Instead monkeys range from the majestic mandrill, with its bright blue fur and coloured face, to the pygmy marmoset, a monkey so small that it can sit in the palm of your hand.

Prosimians – The First Primates

The earliest primates roamed the world about 25 million years before monkeys evolved. They were the prosimians – which means 'pre-monkeys'. Amazingly, there are still many species of prosimians alive today, including aye-ayes, bush babies, lemurs, lorises and tarsiers.

The prosimians' hands mark them out as primates. They have flexible fingers, and thumbs that work in the opposite direction, making it possible for them to hold and pick things up.

Prosimians rely heavily on their sense of smell to communicate and to find food. The advanced primates – the monkeys and apes – use their sight more. In areas where monkeys and prosimians lived together and competed for the same food, the monkeys were more successful and so prosimians had to develop specialized tactics to survive.

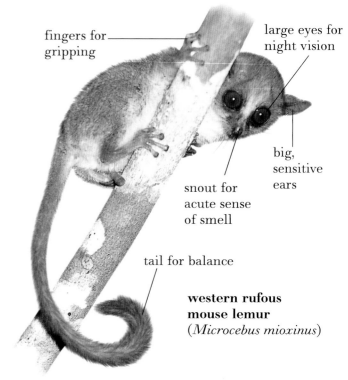

fingers for gripping

large eyes for night vision

snout for acute sense of smell

big, sensitive ears

tail for balance

western rufous mouse lemur (*Microcebus mioxinus*)

▲ **TYPICAL PROSIMIAN**
This lemur is the smallest primate of all. It weighs only 30g, about the same as a tablespoonful of sugar. Lemurs have characteristics common to all prosimians, but are a distinct group of their own. They live only on the island of Madagascar. Monkeys never crossed the sea to the island once it was cut off from Africa 100 million years ago, so prosimian lemurs survived and evolved into many different species.

EXCLUSIVE OLD WORLDERS ▶
Prosimians live only in parts of Asia and Africa. No species are found in the Americas or in Australia. Bush babies and lorises are found in Central and southern Africa. Lemurs live off the east coast of Africa, in Madagascar. The islands and peninsulas of South-east Asia are home to lorises and tarsiers.

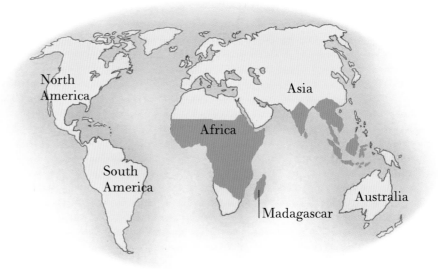

North America

Asia

Africa

South America

Madagascar

Australia

◄ USING YOUR EYES

Despite its goggle-eyed appearance, the tarsier from South-east Asia, is more closely related to monkeys than to other prosimians. Most prosimians rely heavily on their sense of smell to communicate and find food. With the tarsier, however, eyesight has become more important. It can swivel its head 180 degrees in each direction to look over its back.

▲ NIGHTWATCH

Bush babies, or galagos, are nocturnal. In daytime, they snuggle up with their family. Some prosimians survived after monkeys evolved by becoming nocturnal and feeding when the monkeys slept. Bush babies live in African forests, feeding on fruit and insects. This South African galago is only about 16cm (a relaxed adult handspan) long, but it can leap up to 5m.

SCENTED PATH ►

Like other prosimians, the slow loris from South-east Asia stakes out its territory with scent. It rubs urine on its hands and feet so that it can imprint its smell exactly where it wants. It also uses the smell to mark its path. The loris moves slowly to avoid attracting attention from predators in the forest. If something frightens it, the loris can easily return to the safety of its nest by following the scented path.

Did you know? Bush babies can grip tightly to a branch for hours without getting tired.

◄ SOCIAL LEMURS

Ring-tailed lemurs are almost as versatile as monkeys. They are agile climbers, and scamper like cats on the ground. They live in large groups, in which females do all the leading and fighting for dominance. Male ring-tailed lemurs fight only over females.

Monkeys Take Over

In the fierce, overcrowded world of the ancient forests, monkeys had many advantages over prosimians. They had bigger brains and keener eyesight, which enabled them to adapt to different habitats and conditions.

Apes and monkeys evolved around 35 million years ago. At first, apes dominated the forests, but the versatile monkeys soon reigned supreme because they could access foods all over the forest, from the top to the bottom. Because of this, monkeys are still generally built for life in the trees. Most species continue to inhabit warm, wet forests around the Equator, although some have adapted to life on the ground, in desert scrub, on mountains, or even in bustling cities.

▲ DOWN TO EARTH

Unlike many monkey species, baboons do not live in trees. This olive baboon, which lives in grassland, is typical. Baboons are Old World monkeys, mostly from Africa. They live in large social groups that are among the most complicated and interesting of all monkey societies. All four baboon species are bigger than most monkeys.

◄ OLD WORLDS AND NEW

Monkeys evolved in Africa, and spread to the Americas and Asia. The monkey populations on each side of the ocean developed in different ways. Those that remained in Africa and Asia became known as the Old World monkeys. They evolved into many different species but all have narrow noses and downward-pointing nostrils. The American, or New World, monkeys have wider noses with outward-facing nostrils.

North America

Asia

Africa

South America

Australia

◀ NEW WORLD NOSE STYLE

Like all other monkeys that evolved in the New World, this cotton top tamarin has a flat nose with outward-facing nostrils. New World monkeys live in the forests of Central and South America. Most of them have tails that, unlike those of Old World monkeys, can wrap around and grip on to things, and are used as an extra limb.

tail usually longer than body

forward-facing eyes

long, flexible spine

sitting pads – on Old World monkeys only

WALKING FRAME ▶

This Old World monkey from India has many characteristics that are common to all monkeys. Long, slender limbs of about equal length make for easy walking on all fours. Tails are long and flexible – especially on New World monkeys. Hands and feet are designed for climbing, walking on the ground and holding leaves and fruits.

deep, flat chest

long, slender limbs with five-digit hands and feet

hanuman langur
(*Semnopithecus entellus*)

Did you know? Monkeys usually have ridged palms to help them grip on to trees.

OLD WORLD PORTRAIT ▶

Look at the downward-pointing, closely spaced nostrils of this pig-tailed macaque. They are typical features of an Old World monkey. These monkeys are more closely related to the great apes such as gorillas and chimpanzees that also live in the Old World. The wide space between lip and nose is typical of many monkeys and apes but unlikely to be seen on prosimians.

The Last

One particular group of prosimians flourished in just one place in the world. They were the lemurs of Madagascar. Millions of years ago the island split away from the east coast of Africa, leaving its population of prosimians to evolve separately from those on the mainland. With no competition from monkeys and apes, the lemurs of Madagascar evolved into many different species. Today there are around 40, from the tiny mouse lemur to the athletic sifakas and indris, which are about the weight of a medium-sized monkey. Once people arrived on Madagascar, many species of lemur became extinct, including a huge gorilla-sized lemur.

GHOST DANCE

A sifaka hops daintily over open ground. It spends most of its time leaping athletically through the springy leaves of cactus-like trees. When humans first came to Madagascar, they heard the eerie calls of sifaka troops, glimpsed the white-furred figures and thought that the island was haunted. The animals became known as *lemures* — Latin for "spirits of the dead".

ENJOYING THE NIGHTLIFE

The weasel lemur feeds only at night and has a solitary nature, like most of the smaller lemur species. A couple of times a night, a male and female might meet up and groom each other. Most small lemurs eat insects, seeds, gums and fruit. Weasel lemurs, however, are specialist leaf-eaters. Their large intestines break down tough, indigestible plant matter. As an extra aid to digestion and to extract every bit of goodness, they sometimes eat their droppings.

of the Lemurs

COOLING OFF

Ring-tailed lemurs bare their chests and splay their legs to lose as much heat as possible in the cool breeze during the day. They are active at night, too, stopping for short breaks every few hours. This helps to keep up their energy levels. These larger lemurs are quite monkey-like in their behaviour. They live in permanent social groups of up to 30, with a female leader. The smaller, nocturnal species tend to lead more solitary lives, like the mainland prosimians.

SOLE SURVIVOR

The aye-aye is the only surviving lemur of its type, and is itself threatened with extinction. It has survived as long as this by being highly specialized – a long middle finger with a claw-like nail hooks out grubs from wood, or the pulp from fruit, as in this picture. Aye-ayes are very secretive and move about only at night. During the day, they curl up in a nest of leaves.

HIGH-LEVEL LIVING

Ruffed lemurs rarely touch the ground. Their short legs are more suited to running and jumping through the trees than to climbing like the longer-limbed sifakas and indris. As they eat more fruit than other lemurs, they do a useful job of spreading seeds via their droppings. All lemurs, and the ruffed lemur in particular, have a snout like that of a wild dog. This provides more surface area for picking up smells.

71

Outward Appearances

Monkeys and prosimians became experts in forest survival. As different species evolved, each adapting to a particular way of life, a great variety of shapes and sizes emerged. All, however, had the primate speciality of flexible hands and fingers. Thumbs work in the opposite direction to the fingers so that the digits can close together and grasp. Long arms and legs are geared for climbing. On many species the arms and legs are of similar length – which means the animals can walk comfortably on all fours. On others, strong hind legs provide power for leaping. These primates can stand or sit on their haunches, leaving both hands free.

▲ **UNDER THE THUMB**
The pygmy marmoset from South America is small enough to fit on the palm of your hand. It is only about 30cm from its head to the tip of its tail, and weighs about 100g – 500 times less than a mandrill.

▼ **BIG AND BULKY**
Male mandrills are the world's biggest monkeys. They weigh 50kg, about the same as a small adult human. Mandrills walk on all fours and have limbs of roughly the same length. They do not live in trees so they don't need a tail.

▲ **THE FIFTH LIMB**
A black-handed spider monkey has a muscular tail that can wrap around a branch. A hairless stretch of ridged skin on the underside gives extra grip, like the ridges on the palm of a primate hand. Only New World monkeys have tails with this prehensile (grasping) power. The tails of prosimians and Old World monkeys simply help to balance them when leaping through the trees.

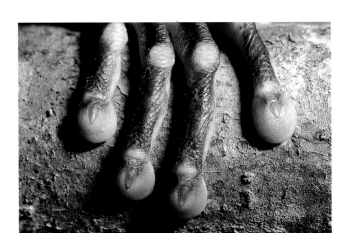

▲ HANDS ON

The long, flexible fingers of the tarsier are padded for extra grip when climbing. The tarsier is a prosimian from South-east Asia. As with almost all primates, it has fingernails. For animals that forage for plant food, fingernails are more useful than claws. They can be used for picking, peeling and gouging as well as for scratching and grooming.

▲ GETTING A GRIP

A young vervet makes the most of its hands and feet to climb. Its opposing thumbs curve in to help it grip. Balanced securely on two feet and one hand, the monkey has one hand free for eating. Monkey hands need to hold small items, so tend to be smaller and more flexible than their feet.

◄ PROBLEM HAIR AND SKIN

A rhesus macaque pulls ticks from her friend. The fur of monkeys is home to many tiny insects that suck the host's blood or make the skin flaky. Monkeys deal with the problem by grooming each other. Grooming is also an important way of making friends. Monkey skin darkens with age because of the effects of sunlight and so many monkeys avoid spending too much time in the sun.

A HANDY FUR COAT ►

For a new-born chacma baboon, mother's fur is handy to cling on to. In the sun-baked savannas, baboons do not need to keep warm, so the baby's fur will become coarse and sparse like its mother's. Fur also gives some necessary protection against the burning sun, and its grey-brown colour provides good camouflage on the African plains.

Inner Power

In terms of brainpower, monkeys and other primates are often considered more 'advanced' than other animals. Their bodies, however, are basically the same as most other mammals. Primates did not develop special physical features like animals that grew hooves or horns.

Small primate bodies are built for flexibility and agility, with hinged joints supported by long, elastic muscles to allow maximum range of movement. Different species have body shapes adapted to whether they climb and leap through trees, or move along the ground. Head shape and size depend on whether brainpower or the sense of smell or sight is top priority. Digestive systems vary according to diet.

▲ DENTAL PRACTICE
Monkeys and prosimians have four types of teeth. There are incisors for cutting, canines for stabbing and ripping, and molars and premolars for grinding tough leaves and fruit into a mushy paste.

▼ INTERNAL VIEW
A monkey's bones and strong muscles protect the vital organs inside its body. Its facial muscles allow it to make expressions. Monkey legs are generally shorter in relation to their bodies than prosimian legs. This gives them more precise climbing and reaching skills, especially in the treetops.

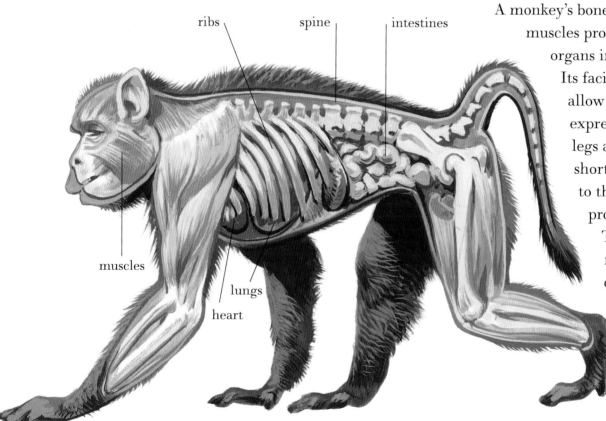

ribs spine intestines

muscles

lungs

heart

▼ BIG EYES

The tarsier has the biggest eyes of any animal in relation to its body size. There is not much room left in its skull for a brain and each of the eyes is heavier than the brain. Prosimians have simpler lives than monkeys and do not need big brains. Instead, they have an array of sharp senses – more sensitive than a monkey's – that help them to survive. As well as its huge eyes, this tarsier has large ears that pick up the slightest sounds in the quiet of the night.

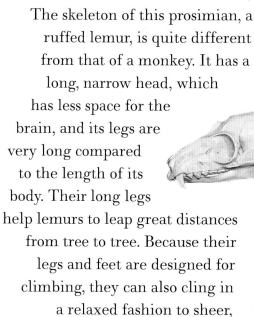

▲ A STRONG STOMACH

A baboon's digestive system can cope with raw meat as well as plant food. Although meat is nutritious, it can be harmful if it stays in the body too long. Meat-eaters have shorter guts than vegetarians, so that food passes through the body quickly. Most monkeys and prosimians eat mainly plants and have longer guts because leaves and other plant foods are hard to digest.

INSIDE LOOK AT A LEMUR ▶

The skeleton of this prosimian, a ruffed lemur, is quite different from that of a monkey. It has a long, narrow head, which has less space for the brain, and its legs are very long compared to the length of its body. Their long legs help lemurs to leap great distances from tree to tree. Because their legs and feet are designed for climbing, they can also cling in a relaxed fashion to sheer, upright tree trunks.

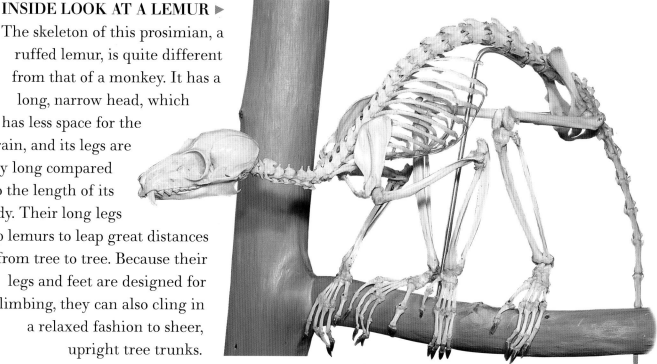

Sensing the Surroundings

Monkeys are usually active in the daytime, and make the most of their excellent colour vision. Most prosimians are nocturnal, and have eyes to help them see at night. The eyes of all primates are lined with a combination of cone cells and rod cells. Monkeys have more colour-sensitive cone cells. Prosimians have plenty of rod cells, designed to see in dim light. Their eyes glow in the dark like cats' eyes because they are backed by a mirror-like layer that reflects every bit of available light.

Sight is very important to monkeys, but prosimians rely much more on the senses of smell and hearing. The ears of prosimians are constantly on the alert. The slightest rustle in the dark could identify an insect snack or an approaching predator.

▲ COLOUR SELECTION

Thanks to its colour vision, an African vervet monkey can select its favourite flowers when they are at the peak of perfection. Many leaf-eating monkeys have eyes that are particularly sensitive to different shades of green. This means that they can easily identify the fresh green of tender young leaves that are good to eat.

MIDNIGHT MONKEY ▶

Douracouli monkeys are the only nocturnal monkeys. They live in South America where there are no prosimians to compete with. Like prosimians, their eyes are big to catch maximum light. They are able to pick up detail but not colour.

▲ EYES LIKE SAUCERS

Unlike the eyes of many prosimians, tarsier's eyes have no reflective layer, but their size means they catch as much light as possible. Like monkeys, their eyes have a sensitive area called the fovea, which picks out very sharp detail.

▼ A KEEN SENSE OF SMELL

An emperor tamarin monkey marks its territory with scent. New World monkeys and prosimians have a smelling organ in the roof of their mouths that Old World monkeys do not have. They use their sense of smell to communicate with each other and to identify food that is good and ready to eat.

▼ MUFFLED SENSE OF HEARING

The furry ears of squirrel monkeys probably muffle sound. But although these and other monkeys use sound to communicate with each other, hearing is not as important for them as keen eyesight. Nocturnal primates, however, have highly sensitive, delicate-skinned ears.

▲ WET-NOSED SMELLING AIDS

Look at the shiny nose of this ruffed lemur. It is more like that of a cat or dog than a monkey. Most prosimians have this moist nostril and lip area, called the rhinarium. It gives them a better sense of smell. The nose has a layer of sensitive cells to detect chemicals in the air. The cells work better when they are wet.

On the Move

Primates are the most versatile movers of the animal world. Many can walk and run, climb and swim. Small monkeys and the larger lemurs can leap between branches. This method is risky for larger animals, in case a branch breaks beneath their weight. Heavier primates play safe by walking along branches on all fours and avoid jumping if possible.

When branches are bendy, climbers move with caution. They may use their weight to swing from one handhold to the next, but they do not let go of one handhold until the other is in place.

Tree-climbing monkeys have long fingers to curl around branches and help them to grip. Monkeys that live on the ground use their hands as well as their feet to propel themselves along the ground.

Did you know? A spider monkey's tail is so strong it can support the monkey's entire weight.

spider monkey
(*Ateles geoffroyanus*)

◀ **CLIMBING POWER**
New World monkeys rarely move at ground level. They swing from tree to tree, stop and whip their tail around a branch, let go with both hands and grab something to eat. Old World monkeys do not have a prehensile (grasping) tail. Many have lost their tails altogether or have very short ones, which they use to help balance in the trees.

◀ **PADDED MITTS**
The palm of a sifaka lemur is just one of the features that makes it a star jumper. The wrinkles and flesh pads are like a baseball glove, giving extra holding power. Sifakas can push off from their long hind legs to leap up to 5m high. Their arms are short, making it impossible to walk on all fours. Instead, sifakas hop on both feet.

◄ BABOONS ON THE MOVE

A troop of baboons makes its way down a track in the African savanna. They are strong and tough because they have to walk long distances to find enough food to feed the troop. Baboons and other monkeys that walk on the ground, such as mandrills, geladas and macaques, put their weight on the fingertips and palms of their hands and feet. This is different from apes, such as gorillas and chimpanzees, who walk on their knuckles.

▲ SLENDER LORIS

Lorises from Sri Lanka and southern India are known for their slow, deliberate movements. They have long, thin arms and legs with very flexible ankles and wrists. A loris can wriggle its way through and get a grip on dense twigs and small branches. Due to its strange appearance, some people describe the animal as a banana on stilts.

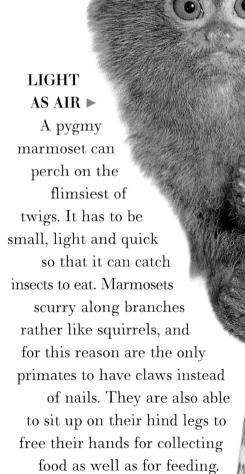

LIGHT AS AIR ►

A pygmy marmoset can perch on the flimsiest of twigs. It has to be small, light and quick so that it can catch insects to eat. Marmosets scurry along branches rather like squirrels, and for this reason are the only primates to have claws instead of nails. They are also able to sit up on their hind legs to free their hands for collecting food as well as for feeding.

79

The Fast,

Long limbs, strong back muscles and a super-long tail make langurs the supreme all-round athletes of the monkey world. They are masters of balance, suspension and speed; as agile on the ground as at the very top of a forest canopy. They can leap farther than most other monkeys, and spend up to 70 per cent of their time moving around the trees.

Langurs live in big troops in south Asian countries, such as Bangladesh, India and Bhutan. The males in a troop try bossing the females around, but the females are really in charge of everything apart from mating. The females also help each other out by sharing childcare.

COMING TO GROUND
A golden langur sits and waits for other members of the troop. Gatherings usually occur in the mornings. They take place on or close to the ground, as there is more space than in the trees.

CLING ON
Long limbs make langurs great at rope-climbing — or in this case climbing a liana (trailing plant). Where trees are more spaced out, langurs are happy to move at ground level. If danger arises, they can speed overland at around 40km/hour.

BALANCING ACT
A langur reaches out to grab some flowers. The branch sways precariously, but the langur is perfectly balanced. Its heavy tail hangs like a plumb weight beneath to secure its position. Langurs have a vegetarian diet of fruits, flowers, berries, shoots and leaves.

Acrobatic Langurs

WELL SPOTTED

Juicy fruit on a neighbouring tree has caught this golden langur's eye. A super-sensitive patch on each retina enables it to focus sharply. The langur's vision also helps it to measure distances for leaping. Their eyes are almost identical in strength and ability to human eyes.

LEAPING FROM TREE TO TREE

As they fly from one tree to another, langurs whoop to other members of the troop to follow. They can leap or drop a dizzying 20m – the height of a two-storey house. Brainpower combined with learning when young, by watching older members of the troop, mean that the monkeys judge distances very accurately.

TIGHTROPE WALKING

A langur walks along a long branch on its hands and feet in the same way it would if it was on solid ground. The monkeys find it easy to do this because they spend so much of their time in the trees.

Brainpower

To survive in the complicated world of forest branches, monkeys developed intelligence. They have excellent hand–eye co-ordination to make the most of their grasping hands and forward-facing eyes. In the forest, monkeys move fast and make split-second decisions such as: "Will that branch hold my weight?" They can work out what the likely effect of their actions might be.

As they live in groups, monkeys have developed their brainpower so that they can negotiate with each other. Another skill for group living is a good memory, and monkeys are certainly good at remembering things. They rely on their memory to identify areas where they found last year's choicest food supplies.

◀ **PROSIMIAN TEAM**
Prosimians that are active in the day, such as these ring-tailed lemurs, are usually cleverer than nocturnal prosimians. Like monkeys, they live in groups and have to work together to control territory and find food.

▼ **THE EVIDENCE FOR INTELLIGENCE**
The skull of a sifaka (*below*) has little brain space, even though it is probably the most intelligent prosimian. The brain makes up less than half the length of the sifaka's skull. The front section – the nose – is long, which reflects the importance of the sifaka's sense of smell. The vervet monkey skull (*right*) is a different shape, with a much larger area behind its eye sockets for the brain.

Monkey Dance
In Mexico, people dress up as monkeys for some traditional dances. The Mayans believed that when the world began, monkeys were types of humans. The monkeys fled to live high in trees because they were tired of being laughed at by other humans.

▲ FINE JUDGEMENT

Thanks to its large brain, this red colobus monkey can make death-defying leaps with absolute precision. Even on jumps of over 20m – the length of a tennis court – it can work out that the jump is possible and where to land safely. The monkey's sense of sight is also vital for gauging the distance between take-off and landing.

▲ LOOK AND LEARN

Toque macaques probably learned to raid rubbish bins for food by watching humans. Their big monkey brains give them the capacity to learn. This ability to learn means that monkeys can adapt to new environments. Macaques have worked out how to survive in a greater variety of habitats than any other monkey.

▲ SOCIAL CONSCIENCE

The members of this troop of chacma baboons all know each other very well. Because they are intelligent, each baboon can remember how other baboons have behaved and reacted in the past. As a result some are good friends, while others are not so close. Some baboons are even enemies. A monkey's intelligence means that it can live in complicated societies like this.

▲ LIMITED NEEDS, SMALL BRAIN

Most prosimians do not need to move and think quickly. They do not have the stimulation of group living, so they do not need as big a brain as a monkey.

Changing Habitats

Nearly all monkeys and prosimians live in steamy rainforests, like their early ancestors. Many monkeys may never touch the ground. Some live right at the top of the tallest trees, leaping from branch to branch. Others live lower down, where branches are so thick that they form an almost solid platform. Species that live in the forest understorey are agile both on the ground and in the trees.

Ground-based baboons and monkeys evolved later than the forest-dwellers. Sometimes, they live far from forests. There are fewer species and smaller social groups in open areas than in the forest, as food is more scarce.

▲ GROUND-BASED

Gelada baboons come from the open grasslands in the Ethiopian highlands in Africa. They are the only monkeys that eat mostly grass, and they live in groups for safety from predators. Like other ground-based monkeys, they have stout bodies for walking long distances in search of food.

Did you know? Some lemurs don't eat in the dry season, living off the fat they store in their tails.

EXTREME VERSATILITY ▶

A Tibetan macaque has a thick winter coat and must rest more than other monkeys to save energy for keeping warm. It gets very cold high in the mountains and food is scarce. The macaques grow thick winter coats to trap heat. Macaques are among the most adaptable of monkeys. Different species have learned to survive farther north than any other monkey, in mountain forests and in cities.

Monkey Gods
Black-faced langurs
are named after the
Hindu monkey
god, Hanuman.
According to legend,
Hanuman stole a
mango plant and faced punishment by fire. When
the fire was lit, the god tried to put it out. His face
and paws were burnt in the process. According to the
story, this is why hanuman langurs have black faces
and paws. Although the monkeys are often pests in
modern India, they are considered sacred. On the
feast day of the god Hanuman, the monkeys are fed
offerings at Hindu temples.

▲ LIFE IN THE FOREST

A baby squirrel monkey hitches a ride on an adult. These monkeys are part of a big troop on a fruit-hunting expedition through the lower levels of the trees. Because there is such a rich variety of food all year round, large numbers of monkeys live in the tropical forests.

◄ POISONOUS SNACK

The favourite food of the rare golden bamboo lemur is a variety of giant bamboo that contains enough cyanide to kill almost any other animal. These lemurs eat only bamboo and live only where they can find it, in the forests of south-eastern Madagascar.

ADAPT AND SURVIVE ►

De Brazza's guenons are excellent swimmers and have carved out a niche for themselves in dense, flooded rainforests in Africa, often on islands. Guenons are one of the most varied monkey species. Most are tree-living, but some, such as the vervet, have adapted to life on the African plains.

Survivors

In the forested mountains in the north of Japan, winter temperatures can drop to -15°C. Japanese macaques have learned to survive farther north and in colder weather than any other primate – except people, of course. Local people call them 'the snow monkeys'. Macaques are generally well known for their ability to adapt and pick up new survival skills. Snow monkeys have learned to make the most of local resources, such as hot springs, and of any food that is available in each season. They live in groups and rarely fight among themselves – for that would waste precious energy. Some migrate south from the very coldest parts of the country.

1 In autumn, the snow monkey feeds on fruit, such as apples. In spring, there are plenty of shoots and young leaves. Then as summer comes, the monkeys can feast on flowers and insects.

2 As winter draws near, the monkeys' fur thickens. Long, fine hairs trap body heat close to the skin like a cosy blanket. Farther south, where winters are milder, the monkeys have lighter winter coats.

3 Some snow monkey troops move south when the winter snows come, but this snow monkey braves it out. They mate three months later than their southern relations, so that the young are not born until late spring. Then the mothers have plenty to eat and can provide milk for the babies.

in the Snow

4 A snow monkey eats bark stripped from a tree. It will also feed on tree buds and seeds, if it can find any. In the very coldest areas, snow monkeys only find about half the food they need to stay alive in the winter months. The rest of the nutrition their bodies need comes from fat stores built up during the previous summer.

6 Japanese macaques cannot sleep in the water, so they have to get out when they are tired. To stay warm, the monkeys huddle into large groups. Together, their bodies lose heat more slowly during the icy nights. Long hairs on the outside of the monkeys' coats prevent snow from reaching their skin and keep them dry.

5 One of the ways in which snow monkeys are able to survive the extreme cold is by having a hot bath. Some years ago, scientists observed a few monkeys taking a trial bath in a hot volcanic spring. Others in the troop followed suit, and now it is a regular snow monkey habit. Because they are using less energy to stay warm, they are conserving vital stores of fat.

Diets for Living

Very few small primates eat just one type of food. Most eat whatever's available through the seasons. Some species, such as mandrills and baboons, range over a wide territory to find enough food to feed the troop. Some become specialists, such as the leaf-eating colobus monkeys of Africa and Asia. They have sharp molar teeth to chop the leaves finely, and extra-big stomachs to extract as much goodness as possible from the tough fibres. Most monkeys eat a varied diet of fruit, nuts and insects, and a few eat eggs and small animals. In general, small monkeys eat more high-energy foods than larger monkeys because they burn up energy faster and need more efficient fuel.

▲ CLEAN FOOD
A Japanese macaque washes meat before eating it. It does not understand that unclean meat may make it ill, but knows that dirt spoils the taste. Once one monkey started to wash food, others in the group copied it. The habit will be passed on to their children. Other troops have not learned to do this.

▲ LAID-BACK EATERS
Red colobus monkeys usually eat leaves, although they also like flowers and fruits. Colobus monkeys do not need to look far for food as leaves are plentiful. They spend a long time sitting still, digesting the leaves to make the most of the limited goodness in them.

▲ SAP EXTRACTION
A bare-faced tamarin licks the thick, sweet juice from a fruit. Tamarins and their marmoset cousins eat a lot of resin from trees, including liquid rubber. Marmosets have pointed bottom teeth with which they pierce the bark so that the liquid flows out.

Greedy Monkey

A fable from Pakistan tells of a monkey that found some wheat inside a small hollow in a rock. The monkey thrust in its hand and filled it with the grain. The opening was too narrow for it to pull out its hand without letting go of some of the food. The monkey was too greedy to let go of any of the food, with the result that it had no food at all.

▲ BABOON ATTACK

A male olive baboon normally eats seeds, insects and grasses, but will not refuse the carcass of a baby animal. This African antelope fell victim to a baboon troop. The monkeys edge toward a herd until a young, weak animal is isolated. Then they rip it to shreds.

▼ SAVING FOR LATER

A drill has filled its cheek pouches with chewed food. Some other Old World monkeys have this habit too. They do this when they are eating leaves so that chemicals in the monkeys' spit begin to break the leaves down. The monkey's stomach will be able to absorb the nutrients more easily from the resulting mush.

▲ EAT UP YOUR PETALS

Flowers are a good supply of food, as this ring-tailed lemur is discovering. The pollen has a higher concentration of protein than any other part of the plant. Many insects are also attracted to flowers, and they are another good source of protein for monkeys and prosimians.

Sharing Space

When monkeys evolved, many prosimians became extinct, because the two groups of animals were competing for the same food. One way to survive in such circumstances is to become a specialist in a particular environment. Gradually, different species of monkeys and prosimians evolved that were able to share space in the same patch of forest. They had different diets, ate at different times, or operated at different levels in the trees.

Monkeys also share the forest with many other animals and plants. Together they make up an ecosystem. If an imbalance occurs in any part of the ecosystem, everything is affected. Too many leaf-eating monkeys living in one area, for example, might strip a tree of its leaves. Both the tree and all the insects that rely on it then die, and the leaf-eaters, as well as any insect-eating monkeys, lose their food supply.

◄ **MY PATCH!**
All species of the South American dusky titi monkey eat seeds and fruits. Each one, though, feeds at a different level of the forest. They do not compete with each other, but may be chased from food by larger monkeys. When this happens, dusky titis switch to eating leaves.

◄ **OPPORTUNISTS**
Baboons are the only monkeys to live on the dry, open grasslands of Africa. They have adapted to eating anything they can find — even grass. The monkeys share the savanna with grazing animals such as wildebeest. There are no other monkeys here as there is not enough food. Even the baboons have to walk a long way each day to find enough to eat.

▲ SECURITY SERVICE

This pig-like animal is a peccary from South America. Peccaries are often found living close to monkeys, to the benefit of both. The hogs root around the bases of trees, feeding on insects, roots and whatever monkeys may drop from the branches. In return, peccaries will attack snakes heading up the trunk, which may be after small monkeys.

▲ MIDNIGHT FEAST

Night monkeys live in the same parts of the South American forest as other types of monkey. They eat many of the same foods, but feed at night, so do not compete. In the same way, nocturnal prosimians can hold their own against monkeys in the same forest.

SPECIALIST LEAF-EATER ▶

A black howler monkey feeds on its main diet of leaves in the South American rainforest. As the only leaf-eaters, troops of howlers can share space with fruit- or insect-eating monkeys. However, other monkeys tend to give the large, noisy howlers a wide berth.

▼ MILITARY TACTICS

Sharing space means developing self-protection. Baboon troops move in a defensive column with the largest males at the front and back. Females walk in the centre with their young. When a predator, such as this leopard, attacks, the males rush forward to fight off the big cat. The females gather with the young baboons at a safe distance.

▲ **CALLING CARD**
The female leader of a troop of ring-tailed lemurs from Madagascar marks her territory with scent from a gland on her chest. In ring-tailed lemur society, it is the females who fight to defend territory. Male lemurs fight only over females.

Territorial Rights

Troops of monkeys spend their lives in one clearly defined area. They create mental maps of their territories, knowing exactly where seasonal food supplies are, for example. Monkeys and social prosimians, such as sifakas and ring-tailed lemurs, defend their territory from neighbouring bands. These group-living primates mark their territory with scent and fiercely defend it against rivals of the same species who may be looking for more space or better food.

Small nocturnal prosimians live solitary lives and do not worry when a neighbour crosses their patch. They are more likely to mate with it or even ignore it altogether.

A primate's territory varies in size according to how many other animals there are and on food supply. A rainforest rich in food can support many animals in small territories. On the plains, animals need to range over a wide area to find enough food.

◄ **FOREST RANGERS**
Squirrel monkeys live in large societies of up to 50 members. Groups move around a home range of 20km², but territorial boundaries are blurred. One troop may merge with another without a hint of a fight. These bands of monkeys have no permanent troops, leaders or clearly defined territories. They roam through the South American forest looking for fruit and keeping track of each other by high-pitched calling.

◀ ON THE MOVE
Baboons live on the African savanna where food supplies are very spread out. They live in big troops of up to 150 animals. This gives them the power to defend massive territories of 40km². The monkeys walk about 5km each day to collect enough food for the troop. Most other monkeys move through only a few trees each day.

UNITED WE STAND ▶
Langurs live in large troops that are controlled by a single male. They patrol big home ranges throughout India, but do not live in rainforests. The troop's leader is always wary of attack from rival males wishing to steal his females and land. The whole langur troop may become involved in a battle with neighbouring troops for control of territory.

◀ KEEP OFF MY LAND
A howler monkey gives a loud, roaring howl warning other troops to keep out of their territory. Both males and females make this noise, and fight off invaders. In the thick forest, sound is a more effective way to assert territorial rights than scent. Fiercely defensive species, such as howler and proboscis monkeys, are the noisiest monkeys of all. The males are the most aggressive, as they also fight for the right to mate with females.

Trumpeters of

LAZY DAYS
This family group of proboscis monkeys spends most of its day eating, high in the trees. They do take time off, though, to groom and to play with each other.

THE PROTECTOR
A male takes up a prominent position to watch out for rival males who may try to steal his harem. Male proboscis monkeys are nearly twice the size of females so that they can look as tough as possible to other males.

If you are a male proboscis monkey, the larger and more bulbous your nose, the better. It makes you look more fearsome to a rival male and it impresses the females. Most importantly, it swells the volume of your territorial honking sounds.

A single dominant male proboscis monkey controls a group of several females and their young. Bachelor males live in separate bands. They all make a lot of noise, screaming, growling and shrieking to each other.

The monkeys spend most of their time in the upper branches, feeding on various leaves, fruits and seeds.

SAFE AND SOUND
Females do not defend territory or fight. They have smaller proboscemarks (noses). Newborn babies have bright blue faces to alert other members of the troop to look after them. As they grow up and fend for themselves, their faces take on adult colours.

the Swamps

LOUD AND CLEAR

An adult male honks loudly to announce his territorial rights. Inside the enormous nose are hollow spaces that act like loudspeakers. As he honks, his proboscis (nose) straightens and stiffens. The sound echoes around the spaces and is amplified (made louder) so that it travels farther through the forest. The males also honk to frighten away predators, and snort to keep the family group in order.

DANGEROUS CROSSING

A proboscis monkey makes a solo voyage through water. Proboscis monkeys have to be very good swimmers because their territory is laced with rivers and inlets. They cross at the narrowest possible point, one at a time, then if a gharial (a type of small crocodile) strikes, it will get only one monkey. It is safer still to find a suitable tree with bouncy branches that the monkeys can use as a springboard to jump across the water.

NOWHERE TO GO

The proboscis monkey's home in the mangrove swamps of Borneo in South-east Asia is being taken over by roads and towns. Many troops are trapped in small islands of mangrove forest with territories too small for their needs. In addition, the coastal plants contain minerals that the monkeys need to stay alive. They cannot survive on similar food that grows inland. Many starve to death.

Predator and Victim

Danger is a way of life for small primates. One false move for a tree-living monkey could mean a long fall to its death on the forest floor. There are hungry predators, too, waiting for a tasty prosimian or monkey.

Small primates that move in the upper branches are in a good position to see any predators approaching from the ground and have plenty of time to move away. However, they are at greater risk from attack by birds of prey, such as eagles. Living in the middle branches offers protection from attack by air and from many ground predators, but tree snakes are a threat. They may spend days waiting motionless for prey to pass close by before striking. Prosimians that shuffle along at ground level by night are in danger from wild cats, silent snakes and swooping owls.

▲ **EAGLE-EYES**
Harpy eagles can swoop between tree branches to grab prey. The South American eagles make nests high in dead, leafless trees. From this exposed position, they watch for food such as monkeys, sloths and birds.

◄ **DANGEROUS CROSSINGS**
In the rivers and lakes of the African grasslands, crocodiles often lie in wait for prey to come near the water. They may snap up a few baboons as troops cross rivers in their quest for food. Swamp monkeys, crab-eating macaques and capuchins spend a lot of time near water and they, too, provide welcome snacks for various local species of crocodiles.

▲ SNAKE IN THE GRASS

A python squeezes the life out of a grey langur monkey. Snakes are a danger to monkeys both on the ground and in the trees. Some snakes squeeze their prey to death, others inject fast-acting venom to kill. Tree-living snakes hold on to their prey as it dies to prevent it from falling out of the branches.

▲ GANG WARFARE

In the African jungle, chimpanzees form hunting parties to attack monkeys such as red colobuses. The monkeys are light and agile, but the chimps are clever and work as a team. One chimp separates a couple of monkeys from the colobus troop and drives them through the forest. Other chimps are stationed nearby to block any escape routes. Chasers force the victims into an ambush, where an old, experienced chimp lies in wait, ready to pounce. Victims are ripped apart in a matter of minutes, and the meat is shared out among the adult chimpanzees in order of importance.

LONE HUNTER ▶

A leopard holds a young baboon in its massive jaws. These predators of the African plains hunt alone. They use stealth to catch their prey off guard, preferring to attack at dusk or at night. The cat often quietly positions itself in a tree or high on some rocks and leaps down on to its prey from above. It will then drag its meal back to the vantage point, where it can eat in peace.

Living Together

All primates communicate in some way with other members of their species, and most of them live in social groups. Community living has advantages. There are more eyes to spot predators, and several animals can work as a team to fight off attack or forage for food. As a community, they stand a better chance of survival if there is a problem with the food supply, during a drought, for instance. The leaders will feed themselves and their young first to make sure that they survive. Solitary animals may have a hard time finding a mate, but within a group, there's plenty of choice. And, when there are young to be cared for, a community can provide many willing helpers.

Nocturnal prosimians rely on being solitary and silent to avoid being noticed by predators. Among bush babies and lorises, even couples live independently of each other, but they occupy the same patch, and their paths often cross. Babies stay with their mother until they are old enough to live alone.

▲ TREE-SHARING
Sifakas work together in groups of about seven adults to defend their territory. They are generally led by the females, and males may switch groups. These prosimians gather in the higher branches of the trees in western Madagascar. If danger threatens, they all start a hiccuping groan.

HAPPY COUPLE ▶
In the jungles of South America, male and female sakis mate and usually live as a couple for a year. The female cares for the young. The father may not spend the day with his family, but does return to them at night. If there is plenty of food, families mingle with each other, forming large, loosely knit groups.

◀ FEMALE RULE

A female is in charge of this troop of black tufted-ear marmosets. As with most other New World marmosets and tamarins, there may be several other females, but only the head female breeds. She mates with all the males to make sure her top-level genes are passed on. As none of the males knows who is the father, they all help rear and protect the young.

EQUAL SOCIETY ▶

The relationship between a woolly monkey mother and her children can last for life. Woolly monkeys live in troops – there may be 20 to 50 of them in each group, with roughly equal numbers of males and females. Adult males often cooperate, and all the males and females can mate with each other. Individual females care for their own young. Woolly monkey groups are bound by an intricate web of relationships between all members that is hard for outsiders to understand.

◀ MALE POWER

These female hamadryas baboons are just two in a harem of several females. One top male mates with all the females to make sure he fathers all the children. Males with no harem live in separate bachelor groups of two or three. They try to mate with a member of the harem when the leader is not looking. When the leader gets old, a few young males will team up to depose him. Once he has been chased away, the victors fight for control of the harem.

Communication

Attracting attention in a noisy forest is a challenge. Groups of tree-living monkeys and prosimians lose sight of each other and keep in touch by calling. Nocturnal prosimians, however, need to keep a low profile, and so leave scent messages, which are easier to place accurately.

All prosimians and, to a lesser extent, monkeys send messages of ownership, aggression or sexual readiness with strong-smelling urine, or scent from special glands. Monkeys can also express their feelings with facial expressions and gestures, and some use their ability to see in colour. African guenons, for example, have brightly coloured patches on their bodies that can be seen by their companions when they are hurtling through the trees. Even fur and tails can be useful. Ring-tailed lemurs swish their tails menacingly at rivals and, at the same time, fan evil smells over them.

▲ DON'T HURT ME

This toque macaque is showing by its posture and expression that it is no threat. If an adult monkey wants to make friends, it may make a sound like a human baby gurgling. The other monkey will usually respond gently.

Did you know? Monkeys have more face muscles than prosimians and make more expressions.

PERSONAL PERFUME ▶

A black spider monkey smears a strong-smelling liquid on a branch. The liquid is produced by a gland on the monkey's chest. Its smell is unique to this monkey. When other monkeys smell it, they know that another of their kind has been there. If they meet the particular monkey that left the scent, they will recognize it.

◄ TELL-TAIL SIGNS

In complicated langur societies, high-ranking males hold their tails higher than lesser members of the group. Primates that live in complex social groups have a wider range of communication skills than solitary species. More information has to be passed around among a greater number of individuals.

▲ YOU SCRATCH MY BACK...

Grooming a fellow monkey not only gets rid of irritating fleas and ticks, but also forges a relationship. A lot of monkey communication is about preventing conflicts among group members. Forming strong personal bonds holds the troop together.

▲ BE CAREFUL

A mandrill has mobile face muscles to make different expressions. Here, he pulls back his gums and snarls. This makes him look very menacing to other males.

▲ I'M ANGRY

When a mandrill becomes angry, he opens his mouth in a wide yawn to show the size of his teeth, and roars. Another monkey will hesitate before confronting this male.

LOOKING FIERCE ►

This marmoset is literally bristling for a fight. Its fur stands on end like an angry cat's to make it look much bigger. It may scare its rival into withdrawing. Marmosets look cute, but they squabble a lot among themselves.

Bright Colours

The startling colours of the male mandrill's face and rump make practical sense. They act like beacons in the gloom of the dense tropical forests of Central Africa. Troops of mandrills roam over large territories of around 50km², so they need to stay in touch with each other.

Groups of about 20 monkeys, made up of a ruling male, several females and more lowly males, may join forces to make armies of up to 250 or more. The monkeys are strongly built, with limbs of equal length for moving around at ground level. At night, they climb into the lower branches of trees to sleep.

LIGHT SNACK
A mandrill spends much of its day rooting for food such as fruit, seeds, or sometimes bird's eggs and small animals. The troop breaks up into small foraging parties to feed.

LOOKING COOL
You can tell that this male is in a relaxed mood, because his colours are quite muted. If he becomes agitated, though, the colours on his broad and boney muzzle flare up. Mandrills are the largest monkeys. The male weighs about 50kg – about the same as a small woman.

MODESTY MOST OF THE TIME
Female mandrills are about half the size of the males, and duller in colour. When ready to mate, a female sends out a colour signal, her bottom swells and turns bright red. Females have one baby at a time. Other members of the troop may help find food for a nursing mother.

of the Mandrills

FOLLOW THE LEADER

All male mandrills have bottoms covered in blue, purple and red skin, with no long tail to reduce the impact of the strong colours. This makes sense in a dark forest, where it is easy to lose the way. Mandrill troops simply spot and follow the colourful male bottoms in front of them. The leading mandrill has the most vividly coloured rump. He also decides when to eat and when to move on. He grunts to announce to the other monkeys when time is up.

BIG TEETH

The male mandrill's vampire-like canine teeth, which are around 6cm long, are nothing to do with its eating habits. Instead they are used as fearsome weapons during fights. The males of a troop of mandrills are constantly fighting to improve their rank, because the top male is the only one who gets to mate with all the females.

CHOOSING A MATE

Female mandrills want their children to be as healthy as possible, so when they look for a mate, they choose a strong male leader. A male's large size and quality of colour are signs of strength and are very attractive to females. This is why males have evolved to look so different from the females. When a male is sexually active, he puts on weight and his colours become more vibrant.

Forming Bonds

From the moment it is born, a monkey must learn to make friends and influence other members of its troop. Without friends, a monkey will get less food and have a harder time rearing its young. Grooming is the social glue that bonds monkey groups together. Monkeys groom each other while they are lazing around, waiting for their food to digest. Grooming is relaxing, and relaxed monkeys are less likely to get into fights. Instead, they work together to find food and raise their young.

Many prosimians use their body scent to avoid confrontations with others. The smells are a signal to other monkeys coming into its territory. Once everyone knows who is in charge in each area, the animals do not get into fights very often.

▲ **MARKING A MESSAGE**
A dominant male lemur marks a branch with a scent gland on his bottom. The other males in the band will smell wherever he's been and make sure they are friendly when they meet him.

◄ **TUG OF LOVE**
The mothering instinct has got the better of the young, inexperienced baboon on the right. She is snatching a baby from its mother. The baby will probably come to no harm, but baby-snatchers sometimes just abandon infants, who then have to be saved by their mums.

PATERNAL INSTINCTS ►
Everyone likes babies, and that's true for monkeys, too. Male monkeys are always jostling with each other for dominance. When an argument gets too much for one male, he may hold up a baby to his rival. Both males forget their disagreements and look after the infant.

▲ SPIDER GROOMING SESSION

A spider monkey checks its friend's fur for lice and ticks. Spider monkeys are very social animals and live in big groups. When resting, these monkeys groom as many other monkeys as they can. If there are too many animals in the group for everyone to groom everyone else, the troop is too large, and the members split up into smaller groups.

▲ GIVING MUM A BREAK

The females in most monkey societies baby-sit for each other. A baby monkey may be suckled by several females as it grows. This tiny grey langur baby is being cared for by an aunt. Young female monkeys learn how to look after babies by caring for their relatives' young.

Did you know? Many monkeys spend almost half their days grooming each other.

HANDS UP FOR GROOMING ▶

A male chacma baboon grooms a female during a break from feeding. Males do a lot of grooming to make sure everyone in the troop likes them. When the breeding season arrives, the females that have enjoyed being groomed by a male will probably be happy to mate with him as well.

◀ LAID-BACK LANGUR

When a monkey is being groomed, its brain releases chemicals, called endorphins, that make the animal very relaxed. Relaxed monkeys are less stressed and will catch fewer diseases, give birth to more babies and be better at avoiding predators. Monkeys will groom even when they are clean and fresh.

A Hamadryas

Male hamadryas baboons are constantly posing threateningly to each other in attempts to win the right to mate with females. The baboons live in small groups known as harems, made up of a single male and several females. All the other males are constantly arguing and fighting to try to take control of another male's harem. The males are more fearsome-looking than the females. They have long manes and dark red faces. Dominant males jealously guard their females, always herding them into a single group.

Hamadryas baboons have adapted to survive in near-desert conditions in Ethiopia and Somalia in Africa, and in southern Arabia on the other side of the Red Sea. They are smaller than other baboons, with brown rather than greyish coats.

TOGETHERNESS
A huddle of females keeps warm in the chilly desert night. The male is at the back on the right. At night, a troop of hundreds of hamadryas baboons may spend the night together for warmth and safety.

CLAN SOCIETY
A female hamadryas baboon rests on a rock. During the day, these monkeys spread out to look for food. The troop divides into smaller groups called clans. A clan is made up of the harems of several related males. Large troops contain two or three clans. Smaller troops have just one. The hamadryas community is the most orderly of all monkey societies.

Baboon Troop

SHOW OF POWER

This is not a yawn of tiredness, but a serious warning to other males not to get too close to this top baboon's harem. Male hamadryas are armed with powerful jaws and long teeth. The layout of their teeth means that the dagger-like canines rub against teeth in the lower jaw, and are kept good and sharp. Like its red face and silver mane, the baboon's teeth are a sign of power.

BANISHMENT

A young male baboon flees from its family group, chased away by its father. As soon as males are old and big enough to be a threat, the top male banishes them from his harem. The young males band together in twos and threes, and join forces to attack a harem in a bid to steal the females. Then they will fight each other for control. The losers of this battle are banished back to the bachelor life.

THE GENTLE SEX

Female hamadryas baboons do not get involved in fights. They spend their time being friendly. They look after the children and groom each other. Most harems have four or five females and their children, but there may sometimes just be a single female. Because they neither compete nor fight, the female baboons are much smaller than the males.

Mating Time

For all animals, mating is a fiercely competitive business. Males want to be sure that it is their genes, rather than those of any other male, that carry on to the next generation. Male monkeys and prosimians fight for the right to mate with females, and bring into play many different strategies to win their favour.

In rainforests, where there is a year-round food supply and the weather is always warm, the young can be cared for at any time of the year. The female primates that live there are able to breed throughout the year. For monkeys and prosimians that live in seasonal climates, however, there may be only one short period in the year when the females are ready to mate. The breeding season has to be timed so that when the young are born there is plenty of food available and the weather is not too extreme.

▲ **FEMALE CHOICE**
Two red-bellied lemurs share a flower. The male, on the left, can be identified by the white patches under his eyes. Among tamarins, marmosets, capuchins and leaf-eating monkeys, it is the females who choose their mates. Tamarins and marmosets lick and hug their chosen mate. Capuchins flirt by raising their eyebrows, and leaf-eating monkeys pucker their lips invitingly.

◄ **FIGHT FOR FEMALES**
The colobus monkey on the left is the dominant male of his society. Only he has the right to mate with his group of females. The dominant monkey is attacking another male who has challenged him. Female colobus monkeys have a short breeding time, so the competition to claim a group of females is intense.

▲ ONCE A YEAR ONLY

Vervets live a comparatively tough life on the savanna. They have longer pregnancies than forest monkeys in the same family, so that the baby develops more in the safety of the womb. Once they are born, the babies have to grow up quickly so that they can learn to look after themselves and not be a burden on their parents.

▲ READY AND WAITING

A female black macaque is ready to breed. Her genitals have swollen into large, red, balloon-like pads. These swellings indicate to a male macaque that she may allow him to mate with her. Many female monkeys have a visual signal like this to show they are ready to mate. Prosimians advertise by scent and calling.

Nazca Monkey

The Nazca people lived in southern Peru about 2,000 years ago. They are famous because they produced a set of huge etchings 120 m long in the deserts in that area. These etchings include pictures of animals, including one of a monkey. Nobody knows why the

Nazca people made these etchings, especially since the pictures cannot be seen from the ground. They were discovered only when an airplane flew over them.

▲ TILL DEATH DO US PART

A woolly lemur family huddles together affectionately in the Madagascan night. These lemurs form strong pair bonds. A male and a female mate only with each other throughout their lives. To keep in touch, they call to each other with long, high-pitched whistles.

Growing Up

Monkeys and lemurs spend a lot of time looking after their young – it is a way of giving them a better chance of survival. In many social groups, adults like to gather around babies. They may find food for the mother, and help look after the child. Langur mothers move away from their troop to give birth. They feed and bond with the baby before introducing it to its relations and friends. All this interaction means that the youngsters soon pick up communication skills. Baby monkeys call out to their mothers in high-pitched voices.

Most primates have only one baby at a time. Nocturnal prosimians tend to have shorter, more frequent pregnancies than monkeys and lemurs. The babies develop less in the womb but grow up quickly after birth. Bush babies start life in a nest, but by nine months are mature enough to have babies of their own.

▲ **CARING FATHER**
Young saddleback tamarins hitch a lift from their father. Because tamarins and marmosets have two or three babies at a time, the fathers get involved in childcare. The children go back to their mother for feeding. Most monkeys have only one baby, which is carried by its mother.

◄ **PLAY AND LEARN**
Young chacma baboons play-fight together. They are learning how to use their growing bodies and practise pulling faces and making noises. They will use these tactics when they are older to threaten enemies or make friends. When young baboons are two or three months old, they start to explore away from their mothers.

◄ HEALTHY DRINK

Baby monkeys start suckling as soon as they are born. The infants of some leaf-eating species are not strong enough to eat solid food until they are 15 months old. Smaller species with more varied diets, such as marmosets, suckle their young for about two months. Lorises, which are nocturnal prosimians of South-east Asia, feed their babies infrequently but with very rich milk, to give the mothers more time to forage for food.

▲ BACHELOR BAND

Young hanuman langur males form gangs and wait for a chance to take over the troop. They have been chased away from the group by their father, the ruling male, because they are a threat to his leadership. In some primate societies that are controlled by a single male, a new leader may kill all the infants because he does not want to look after someone else's children. The females, deprived of their children, are soon ready to breed again and bear the new leader's children.

▲ LOOK AFTER ME!

Adult silver leaf monkeys of the Old World are looking after a couple of youngsters. Other members of a monkey troop may help a mother with childcare. The orange fur of the baby is a signal to the rest of the troop that they must treat the baby very gently. As the monkey grows up, its fur becomes grey and black, like its older friend on the right.

Did you know? Langur mothers hide their young high in trees to protect them from murdering males.

A Young Macaque

1 The newborn baby, a few hours old, is suckled by his mother. She gave birth alone in the early hours of the morning and spent a few hours bonding with her child, before bringing the new baby back to meet her friends in the troop.

Female macaques are pregnant for about five months before giving birth. All the adult females in a troop become pregnant at the same time. The babies are born at the time of year when there is most food.

Although the troop is led by a single dominant male, female macaques each mate with several males. This way, when the babies are born, all the males think they might be their fathers, and everyone works together to look after them.

A young macaque spends most of its time playing with friends. It learns how to express its feelings, and can soon spot when a monkey is angry, happy or hurt. These social skills are essential for adult macaques.

2 The growing macaque clings to his mother. She must feed a lot while she is suckling her baby, so she can make enough milk. Females lose up to one third of their body weight while they are producing milk.

3 Mother and child must follow the troop long distances each day. Now he is bigger, the baby rides all day on his mother's back. That's thirsty work for mum, and while she stops for a drink of water, her son takes a look around. He is just learning to walk, and stumbles and trips close to his mother while she takes a rest or feeds.

Matures

4 For several months the young macaque has taken nothing but his mother's milk. Now he is independent enough to begin to seek out his own food. By his first birthday, the young macaque knows where to find and how to recognize ripe and tasty food. He feeds himself, munching on nuts, fruits and plant shoots.

5 The young macaque is getting increasingly adventurous. Here he sets off to explore a watering hole. However, danger is all around, and he rarely strays far from his mother. Although she probably has a new baby by now, the young macaque will continue to live with his mother until he is four years old.

6 While still with his mother, the macaque begins to make friends with other monkeys. By grooming and being groomed, the young monkey takes his place in the troop. He learns which macaques are in charge, and, while under the watchful eye of his mother, he begins to get involved in the politics of the troop.

7 The macaque is now a fully grown male and he is less and less welcome in the troop. Soon he will have to leave home and set out to find another troop to join. He will need all his social and political skills to be accepted by them. Once in the new troop, he will have to spend a few years being kind to the females, and eventually they will let him father their children.

Monkey Relations

Prosimians, monkeys and apes are all members of the order of animals called primates. Each evolved in turn, adapting first to a life in the trees, and gradually relying on their intelligence to survive. Prosimians and less intelligent monkeys are called lesser primates. The advanced primates, or anthropoids (man-like), are the bigger-brained monkeys and apes. There are 19 ape species (compared with 242 species of monkey). Gibbons, known as the lesser apes, are the largest group and the most monkey-like. The great apes are gorillas, chimpanzees, orang-utans, bonobos and humans. Of all primates, the great apes are the best at holding and manipulating small objects in their hands – and people are the most skilled of all.

KING OF SWING ▶

A lar gibbon swings through the forests of Asia. Gibbons are expert swingers, with arms as long as the rest of their body and legs together. Tails were not necessary for balance and so disappeared. Gibbons look for grubs on the ground, and have to raise their arms in the air to stop them dragging. Male and female gibbons live as a couple for life.

◀ KINDRED SPIRITS

The white back of this gorilla shows he is a full-grown male. Like people, older gorillas, especially males, get white hair. It's a sign of their strength and experience. Gorillas are the largest primates. They are around twice the weight of a well-built adult man, and over 2m tall. The animals live in permanent family groups in the forests of central Africa. Their senses of sight and hearing, and many of their gestures, are similar to ours.

TOO CLEVER BY HALF ▶
Like other apes, humans are descended from the primates that developed in the Old World. People are the most intelligent animals on Earth. As a result, humans can live in any environment. They can shape — and often destroy — the natural world to suit their needs. This young girl is only a few years older than the woolly monkey she is holding, but she has always been cleverer than the monkey.

▲ OLD MAN OF THE FOREST
The people of South-east Asia thought that orang-utans were old men who had left their villages to live quietly in the trees. Orang-utans are the world's largest tree-living animal, and have to climb slowly, choosing the strongest branches. They spend much of their time wandering alone through the forests looking for fruit.

◀ CLEVER PRIMATE
Bonobos are the closest ape relative to humans. They are the only other primate that regularly walks upright. Standing on two legs enables them to see over long distances, reach food on branches and have both arms free so that they can catch fish or hold their young.

▲ LESSONS WITH MOTHER
A chimpanzee baby is dependent on its mother for about five years. It has plenty of time to learn about how to behave in the complicated chimpanzee society. Chimps live in small patches of rainforest in central Africa. They form close relationships with each other and can make and use simple tools. They spend a lot of time on the ground, but climb trees to find fruit and to sleep.

115

Habitat Destruction

▲ TRIBAL PREDATORS

The traditional weapon of hunters in South American forests is a blow pipe. The hunters fire poisoned darts from the long pipe with a quick out-breath. The poison is a paste made from crushed plants or frog skins. In Africa, traditional hunters catch monkeys in nets, or fire arrows from a small bow.

Tribal peoples who live in the tropical rainforests and other wild habitats exist in harmony with monkeys and prosimians. They form part of the natural balance of their environment, along with the plants and other animals. The people take only what they need from their surroundings for building materials, food and medicines, and do not threaten the ecosystem.

On a global scale, though, humans are the world's dominant species and they exploit the Earth's resources for their own ends. They destroy habitats to make room for cities and roads, and for farmland to feed their huge populations. As a result, the habitats of many prosimian and monkey species are either chopped up into fragments too small to support them, or lost altogether. The animals then face extinction.

MONKEY MEAL ▶

A man cooks a monkey in a Central African forest. Traditional hunters do not kill more than they need for their families, so do not threaten the monkey populations. In some parts of the world, however, more and more people want to eat monkey meat. Hunters, armed with guns, kill monkeys for the bush meat trade. If the demand for monkey meat continues to increase, some areas may soon have no wild monkeys left at all.

◄ DEFORESTATION

This barren South American landscape was once thickly forested and home to howler and black squirrel monkeys, and capuchins. The trees were cut and burned to make space for grazing cattle. The ash fertilizes the soil, briefly. Soon, though, without a rich variety of vegetation growing on it, the soil becomes poor and dusty. More forest is then destroyed to make new farmland.

LAST REFUGE ►

These Verreaux's sifaka lemurs are one of many species that are unique to Madagascar. All lemur species are in danger as people cut down vast tracts of forest, mainly for fuel. More than 14 lemur species are known to have become extinct since the humans began settling the island around 2,000 years ago.

▲ TALKING DESTRUCTION

Mobile phones contain a rare metal called tantalum. It is found in only a few places around the world, including Central Africa. Here, where mandrills and mangebeys struggle for survival, people are fighting over control of the tantalum. This has made it very hard to protect the monkeys.

◄ HIGHWAY ROBBERY

A lorry transports logs that have been cleared to make way for a road. Roads and villages in a forest can make it difficult for monkey populations to meet each other. Cut off from one another, they face extinction. Monkeys need to mate with other groups to produce healthy young. They also need to move easily to areas where there is food.

117

Life in a

Monkeys have lived alongside people throughout history. When humans began to farm and settle in communities, monkeys soon learned that there were easy pickings to be had. These monkeys were the generalist (non-specialist) species with a varied diet. Among them were the cheeky capuchins of the New World, the wily macaques of southern Asia and the highly adaptable vervets of Africa.

In many towns and cities there are monkey species that have been urbanized for generations. They have bigger and denser populations than any that exist in the wild.

EASY PICKINGS

A macaque's hands are ideal for foraging among human rubbish. Urban monkeys are clever and adaptable and will eat anything! They watch humans and learn where food supplies may be and how to get at them. They often take just a mouthful before moving on to the next readily available snack.

HUMAN TASTES

Like most urban monkeys, this vervet has developed a taste for human food. In some cities, urban monkeys have become pests and are bold enough to steal from shops and even food cupboards in houses. Tourists from countries where there are no monkeys are fascinated by them and feed them. This encourages the monkeys to scavenge even more.

Concrete Jungle

ALMS FOR THE POOR

In India, one monkey species has become known as the temple macaque, because large numbers of them live around temples. Often, rows of holy men and poor people begging line the roads to the temples. The monkeys have learned to beg, too — for scraps of food from the tourists and worshippers. One of the reasons why macaques and other urban monkeys fit so comfortably into city life is because human society is similar in many ways to how monkey groups live and interact.

ON THE ROCK

Barbary macaques live in Gibraltar, scavenging rubbish and food from tourists. They are the only monkeys to live wild in Europe. Barbary macaques are sometimes confused by the signals from people. They have been known to attack people who smile and stare, because these are aggressive signals in macaque society.

WHERE THERE'S A WILL...

City monkeys, especially vervets, steal food from people's homes. They can open doors, cupboards and boxes containing food. The vervets can be very determined, and will spend a lot of time working out a way to break in, and even brave a shock from an electric fence. People try to protect their homes by putting bars over windows, locking doors or setting up alarms.

Use and Abuse

Humans have often woven magical stories around monkey characters and even worshipped monkey gods. However, they have also captured monkeys and used them cruelly.

By international law, it is illegal to buy and sell monkeys without a licence. This may be given, say, for the purposes of scientific experiments. Unfortunately, some animals are illegally exported, often travelling long distances in cramped and cruel conditions.

Many monkey and ape species are eaten in Africa and South-east Asia. Most are eaten by local people, for whom monkeys are a cheap source of "bush meat". However, more and more monkey meat is being smuggled around the world, especially into Europe and China, where it is sold illegally for very high prices. Conservationists believe that, if the bush meat trade is not stopped, many monkeys and apes could be wiped out within a few years.

▲ AT YOUR SERVICE
In Malaysia, macaques are trained to climb palm trees to pick coconuts. The agile monkeys easily scramble up to the top of the trees, where the coconuts grow. The macaques have learned to throw the coconuts down to their human owner. Although the monkeys are captive, this task is similar to the behaviour of wild macaques.

◄ PERFORMANCE
In parts of Asia, monkeys, such as this rhesus macaque, are trained to perform tricks to earn money for their human owners. Wild animals in captivity are often treated cruelly by being forced to perform in a way that is completely unnatural to them. Monkeys are not domesticated animals that have been bred to live with humans.

▲ OBEYING ORDERS

This monkey has been put in a cage to stop it escaping. The monkey will behave toward its human owner as a low-ranking male would do to a troop leader in the wild: it will cower to avoid confrontation and will try to do what the owner wants in return for access to food.

▲ FOR THE SAKE OF THE HUMAN RACE

Live monkeys are sometimes used in scientific experiments. This is called vivisection. Some of these monkeys are injured or killed. Many scientists believe that vivisection provides important information that could reduce the suffering of human beings, but others disagree.

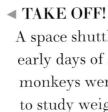

◄ TAKE OFF!

A space shuttle blasts off. In the early days of space travel, many monkeys were used in experiments to study weightlessness.

GUIDE MONKEYS ►

Capuchins – the cleverest New World monkeys – have been taught to help disabled people. The monkeys can pick up objects such as telephones and take them to their owners, as well as perform tasks such as operating switches. Although their owners might benefit, not everyone thinks that it is right to use monkeys in this way.

Saving Species

When the last member of a species dies, that species is extinct. It is lost forever. In the last few decades, some people have worked to stop the rarest primate species becoming extinct. Some have started sanctuaries and zoos where animals are helped to breed away from predators. Nearly half of the world's total population of aye-ayes (one of the most threatened lemurs in Madagascar) is in zoos because there is not enough of their natural habitat left to support them.

To save an endangered species, the cause of the threat must be addressed. This might be the destruction of the animal's habitat or the poverty of the people who hunt them. We can all affect the survival of species by making sure that we do not buy products that cause damage to a monkey's habitat.

▲ LIFE IN A COLD CLIMATE

Woolly monkeys come from the steamy jungles of Brazil. This one lives in English woodland. The monkeys' natural habitat in Brazil is being destroyed by humans and the species is disappearing fast. At their cliff-top home in the south-west of England, the monkeys are given special foods to make sure they get the same minerals in their diet as they would in the wild.

Did you know? Thanks to conservationists, only one primate has become extinct in 100 years.

◀ BACK TO THE WILD

Gerald Durrell, a British conservationist, holds a red-ruffed lemur. Durrell set up a pioneering zoo on the island of Jersey. Many rare primates have been bred there, and the zoo has successfully reintroduced lemurs and tamarins to their natural habitats. The Jersey zoo teaches keepers from other zoos how to raise captive-born animals so they can be released back into the wild.

◀ **HOME FROM HOME**

A rainforest has been created in New York's Bronx Zoo. The temperature, humidity and light are as close as possible to the natural conditions. Captive primates raised in a habitat similar to their wild environment are less likely to become distressed. They will stand a better chance of survival if they are later released into the wild.

KEEPING TRACK ▶

These two golden lion tamarins, born in a zoo, were released into a protected area of Brazilian forest. Scientists fitted them with radio transmitters to keep track of them. This species has been saved from extinction by being bred in zoos around the world.

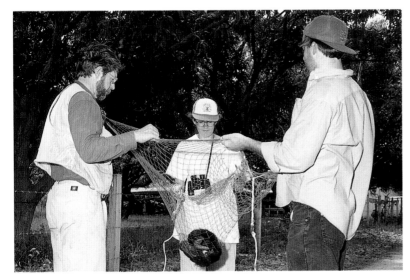

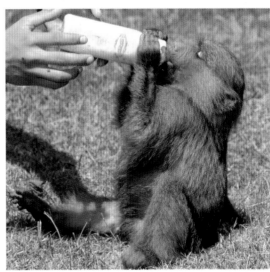

▲ **ONE IN THE BAG**

Scientists have shot a howler monkey with a drugged dart. They will take some measurements then give the monkey another drug to bring it back to consciousness. Their aim is to gain as much information as possible about the howler monkey's population make-up, its diet and the diseases it suffers. This will help them to understand how to conserve the species better.

▲ **SAFE SANCTUARY**

A monkey whose parents were killed by hunters has been rescued and taken to an orphanage. Sometimes, young monkeys that were captured illegally are rescued and sent to zoos to be cared for. They can't be set free as they don't know how to survive in the wild.

GLOSSARY

agile
Moving quickly and easily.

ape
An intelligent primate with no tail, a small nose, long arms and grasping hands and feet. Chimpanzees, gorillas, gibbons, orang-utans, bonobos and humans are all apes.

band
A group of prosimians, such as ring-tailed lemurs, similar to a troop of monkeys.

blackback
An adolescent male gorilla, aged 8-10 years, whose back has not yet turned silver.

bonobo
A great ape that lives in the African rainforests of the Congo. It looks like a chimpanzee and is sometimes called a pygmy chimpanzee.

brachiation
Moving along by swinging from one hand to another beneath a branch, as gibbons do.

camouflage
Colours, patterns or shapes that allow an animal to blend in with its surroundings.

canines
Sharp, pointed teeth that are next to the incisors at the front of a mammal's jaw. Canines are used for piercing and tearing food, and for defence.

carcass
The dead body of an animal.

civil war
A war that is fought between different groups within the same country.

clan
A subgroup of a troop of hamadryas baboons, made up of three or four related male baboons and their harems of females.

community
A large social group of individuals such as chimpanzees or humans, who live together.

conservation (of nature)
Protecting living things and helping them to survive.

deciduous forests
Forests made up of trees that lose their leaves in winter or in a dry season.

diet
The food that an animal eats.

digest
To break down food so it can be absorbed into the body and provide energy.

digit
A finger, thumb or toe.

dominant
A monkey or prosimian that is in charge of, or is dominant in a troop or band.

ecosystem
A group of living things in a certain area that live together and interact with and depend on each other.

endangered species
A species of animal or plant that is likely to die out in the near future.

endorphin
A chemical produced by the brain, which gives an animal a relaxed, contented feeling.

evolution
The process by which living things change gradually over generations.

extinct
When every member of a species of animal or plant is dead.

fermentation
A chemical process that breaks down sugars and starches. Fermentation occurs in the stomachs of animals that eat a lot of plants.

fossils
The preserved remains of living things, usually found in the rocks.

fovea
A patch of highly sensitive cells found at the centre of the retina in the eye. These help monkeys to see clearly.

generalist
An animal that eats all types of food.

gharial
A small type of crocodile found in Asia.

great apes
The four largest apes – chimps, bonobos, gorillas and orang-utans. Humans are also classed, by some, as a great ape.

grooming
The cleaning of an animal's fur, either by itself or by another individual. This calms animals down, helps them to make friends and avoid conflict.

habitat
The place where an animal naturally lives.

harem
A group of females that is controlled by a single male.

home range
An area of land or territory that generally takes an animal or group of animals several weeks or months to move through.

incisors
The cutting teeth of mammals, which are at the front of the jaw.

Jacobson's organ
A small organ at the top of many animals' mouths that helps them to detect smells better. Many prosimians have these organs.

keratin
The protein used to make hair and fingernails.

leader
The monkey or prosimian in charge of the troop, band or harem. Not all primate societies have leaders.

lesser apes
The 11 species of gibbon, which are smaller than the great apes and live in trees all the time. They can move by brachiation and do not build nests.

lowland gorillas
The two subspecies of gorilla (western and eastern lowland gorillas) that live in lowland rainforests of Central Africa.

mammal
An animal with a backbone, fur or hair that can control its own body temperature (and is warm-blooded). Females feed their young on milk made in mammary glands.

mangrove
A type of tropical tree that grows close to water. Mangrove roots hang down from the plant into the water.

mature animal
A fully developed animal that is able to breed.

mineral
A type of chemical that is given in food and is essential for good health.

molars
Chewing and grinding teeth at the side of a mammal's jaw.

monkey
A clever, playful primate with a tail. They usually have a round face and a small nose. Monkeys are active in the daytime and live in groups. Many of them live in trees.

mountain gorilla
A very endangered subspecies of gorilla, with long hair, which lives in the mountains of the Virunga volcanoes (on the borders of the Democratic Republic of Congo, Rwanda and Uganda), and in Uganda's Bwindi-Impenetrable forest.

New World
The name given to North and South America. Monkeys from the New World usually have prehensile tails and flat noses with outward-facing nostrils.

niche
The position a species takes in an ecosystem. It may refer to an animal's diet or the time of day it eats.

nutrient
A part of food that gives an animal energy and good health.

Old World

The name given to Europe, Asia and Africa. Monkeys and prosimians from the Old World usually have tails for balance and small noses with downward-facing nostrils.

opposable digit

A thumb or toe that can touch the fingers or toes in a grasping action, allowing objects to be held firmly.

orbit

The circular part of an animal's skull that holds the eye.

orphan

An animal without any parents.

poaching

Capturing and/or killing animals illegally, usually to sell them for commercial gain.

predator

An animal that catches and kills other animals for food.

prehensile

A part of the body adapted for grasping and gripping. Many monkeys and other mammals have prehensile tails.

prey

An animal that is hunted and killed by other animals.

primates

A group of mammals that includes lemurs, bush-babies, monkeys, apes and humans. Primates are intelligent animals that mainly live in trees and have limbs adapted for climbing, swinging or leaping. They have flexible fingers and toes, and forward-pointing eyes.

proboscis

A long, flexible nose, such as that of the proboscis monkey.

prosimians

The group of primates that includes lemurs, bush-babies, lorises, pottos and tarsiers. Prosimians have smaller brains but a better sense of smell than other primates. They are usually active at night.

pygmy chimpanzee

See bonobo.

quadruped

An animal that walks on four legs.

rainforest

A type of forest that is wet throughout the whole year.

rhinarium

The moist area on some animals' noses that joins the nostrils to the lips. It enhances an animal's sense of smell.

sagittal crest

A large bony crest on the top of the skull in some primates, notably adult male gorillas.

silverback

An adult male gorilla named after the saddle-shaped area of silver hair on his back.

skeleton

A framework of bones inside an animal's body, giving it support and also strength.

social animal

An animal that lives in a group.

solitary animal

An animal that lives alone.

species

A group of animals that can breed with each other and share many similar features. Two animals from different species cannot mate with each other.

submissive animal

An animal that does not occupy an important position in a group and gives way to dominant individuals.

territory

An area of land that one or more animals defend against members of the same and other species.

troop

The name given to a group of monkeys.

venom

Natural poison produced by some reptiles, insects and other animals. These animals use venom to kill their prey and to defend themselves from attackers.

vocal cords

Two folds of skin in the throats of warm-blooded animals, which vibrate and produce sound when air passes over them.

INDEX